It's as easy as a parlor game!
It can change your entire life!
Reading
PERSONALITY SIGNS

- Use your body signals to reach self-realization.
- Use the information gained by observi̶ng others, role-playing signals ̶ ̶ ̶ ̶ ̶ ̶ls.
- Discover the meani̶ ̶ ̶ ̶ ̶ ̶ ̶
- Read the erotic ̶ ̶ ̶ ̶ ̶ ̶
- Sense the under̶ ̶ ̶ ̶ ̶ ̶ by particular t̶ ̶ ̶ ̶ ̶ ̶
- Interpret the "pe̶ ̶ ̶ ̶ ̶ ̶at disturb others and learn̶ ̶ ̶ ̶ey really care about.
- Learn others' compulsions by learning their hobbies.
- See the evidence of security needs in home furnishings.
- Understand what physical problems reveal.

Personality Signs

MAX LÜSCHER

WARNER BOOKS

A Warner Communications Company

WARNER BOOKS EDITION

Copyright © 1981 by Max Lüscher
All rights reserved.

Warner Books, Inc., 75 Rockefeller Plaza, New York, N.Y. 10019

Ⓦ A Warner Communications Company

Printed in the United States of America

First Printing: September, 1981

10 9 8 7 6 5 4 3 2 1

Personality
Signs

Preface

This is the first comprehensive practicable presentation of personality theory based on functional psychology, which came into existence over three decades ago and became the basis of color psychology. Since its inception, it has been employed in conjunction with the Lüscher Color Test in psychosomatic medicine, psychiatry, ethnology, personnel selection, marketing psychology, and in scores of tests and exams in most cultured and civilized nations.

Functional psychology is intelligible simply because it answers, for the reasoning person, the questions most of us confront every day: What am I— and what is the personality of the other person?

To pass up this once-in-a-lifetime chance for self-realization is to deny yourself a means to inner freedom.

I sincerely hope that the pleasure I had in recognizing the issue, and writing about it, will bring you happiness and contentment.

Max Lüscher

Introduction
Personality Signals

"Signals of the personality" is an unusual word combination. But it describes something which we learn and use every day; perhaps without being aware of it, we determine the personality traits, the total person, of people we encounter in flash judgments and from many signs.

We take the word "sign" from the Latin *signum*, meaning sign or signal—for example, a sign post, a stoplight, a uniform, a club emblem, or a framed diploma. They all convey a certain meaning. A person's black hair or oval face are not indicative of personality, although they are symbols by which the person may be recognized or identified. As "signals of personality," I mean the hints and symbols which a person may give out to indicate to others the kind of individual he or she wishes to be taken for. We grasp these signals, however subconsciously, with amazing precision, whether they are being used involuntarily or by design. And, semiconsciously, we understand their hidden intentions and we make daily use of them.

Thus, personality signals are all those mannerisms a person employs to create a specific impression and judgment in his fellow beings. They may be used to make the "signaler" appear superior and self-assured, or naive and helpless.

These ever-changing multiple signals may be as indirect and hidden as psychosomatic complaints— for instance, a feigned heart attack which signals: "because I'm helpless, you have to take care of me." Or they can be as direct and obvious as signals displayed with naive pride. The signals may appear in poses ranging from arrogant pomposity to intentional modesty, or false vanity.

Whoever consciously knows, recognizes, and properly arranges these signals, in order of importance, also understands their motives. That person understands more than words can express, and is hard to confuse. He has the "native intelligence" we attribute to animals, and can judge human nature instinctively.

Once you know and understand what we attempt here, you, too, can "send" these signals, and achieve the exact results you hope for.

Promotion executives and advertising experts commonly earn their bread and butter by properly using these signals. Many others derive great pleasure from deciphering these mysterious signals, in-

interpreting their meaning, and guessing people's relationships. We call this amusing hobby "people watching" or "crowd gazing," though it may be nothing more than idle curiosity.

These attempts to interpret observed signals presuppose that we possess a system by which to classify our observations.

I use the method of functional psychology, on which I also based the color test taken by tens of thousands of subjects in many cultures the world over.

Chapter 1

Realization of the Self

Psychologists are accused—frequently justifiably —of suspecting "something behind everything, and nothing appearing normal, usual, or routine." Psychoanalysis has actually delved into the sickness of mind and soul. To turn psychic health into methodology— actually the concern of pedagogy and philosophy— is a rather difficult task for the mental disciplines of the Occident.

Since a healthy personality is the goal, functional psychology begins with a norm—i.e., with a reality-related disposition of the individual. This goal, personality health, seeks functional psychology as a means to self-realization.

The Scope of Self-Realization

Realization of the self, the greatest opportunity which life offers the individual, is accomplished once we can accept and affirm our present mode of living without any reservations and with conviction of all basics. The adventure of a fulfilled love-relationship or an accomplishment which demands conviction and the use of all our capabilities, are examples of self-realization. We experience them as "bliss." The demands of an individual can be fantastically excessive, absolute, and illusory, or they may be relevant to reality. Demands which relate to reality are never absolute, but rather always dependent on comparison, i.e., relative or comparative to some thing. Whoever accepts an obstacle as real, whoever is ready to "bear his cross," is in touch with reality; that person is ripe, mature. He has found happiness in reality and realism. He has realized himself. Someone who struggles, who loves, who concentrates on reality, forgets himself (i.e., his troubles) is unaware of himself, but he does live in the present and in reality; in truth, with all his senses and sensations.

Self-realization and blissfulness don't fulfill themselves in egocentric self-examination, but rather in the opposite—in an unself-awareness (or self-unawareness), and a healthy relationship to reality..

Signals of Self-Realization

Many psychiatrists are called on every day to determine whether a patient suffers from mental conflicts and disturbances, i.e., a neurosis which can occur in normal individuals, or whether they're encountering an abnormality, a so-called mental illness, i.e., a psychosis such as schizophrenia.

In the case of a psychiatrist being summoned as an expert witness, he must decide whether the accused committed an act as a normal individual or as a person with diminished responsibility. If the individual is either inebriated, psychotic, or feeble-minded while committing an illegal or criminal act, it seems inevitable to conclude that the perpetrator was not normal or fully accountable.

It is confusing that "normalcy" and "average" are so similar in their usage as to assume equal value in many instances. We often object to the attitude which regards only that which the average individual does as normal. The majority of us lead a life full of inner conpulsions and roles acted out quite laboriously. That is not what we perceive as normal life.

Normal and average, concepts which we'd like to separate, cross paths all the time. For example, we speak of our eyesight becoming weaker as a normal sign of old age. But is it "normal" for a person to be blind? Surely not, but in all other respects we consider that person to be normal. Is a brain-damaged child normal? He is most frequently unable to learn how to read and write. And yet he may be sensitive to human relationships. Is the clever businessman normal? He may lack human understanding to such a degree that we speak of him as an emotionally poor or starved person. Then he's comparable to the "unemotional psychopath," who also lacks sympathy, empathy, honor, justice, and shame. Are individuals whose conduct and reasoning change substantially with advanced age or illness still normal, or do we not take them seriously because they no longer "know what they're saying?"

On the average, a person who exploits such a condition is no longer honest. Neither parents nor marriage partners would consider such dishonesty a normal attitude.

In an entire technical realm we speak of norms when we consider units of measurement or size, i.e., a meter as a measurement or a "norm" of a construction element.

Correspondingly, we say that the size of a giant's body, or that of a dwarf, represents a departure from the norm.

Bach, Einstein, Göethe all departed from the average in their cerebral achievements, and yet they were normal. In this case "normal" is absolutely unrelated to "average." Normalcy is measured by how truthful and genuine, how realistic the insight, and how judiciously and sensibly the person behaves.

We judge behavior as normal, or we say of a person that he is "very normal" if his behavior is justified in a given situation. But to *be* this way and to relate to reality, one has to know how to behave properly and correctly. We need a gauge to judge "correctly," we need specific norms and guidelines by which to judge. These are authoritative ideals pointing the way as mental values of measurement (as conscience). These mental norms are targets, ideals a person aims for in order to be able to judge and to act properly.

16

Psychiatrists and sociologists, too, judge the normalcy of an individual by these reference points. If a mother didn't consider it ideal to care for her offspring, she wouldn't be considered normal. If an adult wouldn't regard it as ideal to take care of himself, to feed himself, to walk by himself, to be unaided in his accomplishments, he wouldn't be deemed normal.

An individual who has no manner of ideal could not be regarded as normal.

The Definition of "Normal"

To be called "normal" involves two meanings. Normal in the physical and in the technical sense is to correspond to the average—the norm here is the average. However, something radically different occurs when we equate normalcy with a mental target, an ideal. The ideal as determinant has nothing to do with the average amount. Quantity and average have no part in this. Independent of the person being honest on the average, honesty toward one's fellow man remains an authoritative ideal, an aiming point which serves the normal person in his manner of speech and his behavior.

Because normalcy is not a *value* average but an *ideal*-norm, we cannot explain it quantitatively nor by statistics. Statistic averages give us only sociological data. They do not reveal an insight into the human psyche, nor into the psychic structure of the individual.

If we employ exactly calculated average values

to relate to hypothetical, ambiguous, and imprecise concepts such as "introversion" or "neuroses," we then doubt the scientific value, and these ambiguous concepts become useless to the careful practitioner.

Normalcy, as is used in psychologic judgment and consultation with healthy or disturbed, neurotic individuals, can be measured only by qualitatively defined ideal-norms.

Normalcy, the Ideal of Social Self-Realization

Ideals are a necessity for every person who seeks the meaning of life as a whole. Therefore, ideals have to reveal all possibilities of social self-realization, if they're to embrace the entity of life.

Ideals are directional norms. Like guideposts, they only indicate a direction which we have to choose if we're to realize our inner self. They are not targets we have to hit, but rather, directional signals by which we must orient ourselves. The more consistently we live up to these ideals, the more pronounced is our normalcy, the more genuine our naturalness, and the further we remove ourselves from role-playing and the unnatural compulsions of our society.

Ideologies

Because the "meaning of life" embraces the total of all life's potentiality, every expression of the absolute, of a one-sided ideal, each ideology is therefore illogical. In anarchy, as in all other power-hungry ideologies, this type of antilogic leads to tragic consequences: to the negation of all other ideals, especially tolerance, and to the destruction of all values.

Authoritarian intolerance is thus part of the nature of every ideology. Ideologies tend to interpret the many-sidedness and mutability of reality with absolute and always one-sided idealism. With this principle, ideology explains reality, rationalizes it, and conquers it by the same process. Anarchists (provided we aren't thinking of conflict-burdened and aggressive individuals) regard "social justice" as an absolute, and ignore other social ideals such as tolerance, open-mindedness, sincerity, candor, and benign love. That is the reason such individuals negate all other ideals and dispute their application. Ideologies, whether artistic or theoretically scientific in nature, are therefore authoritarian, and lack tolerance. Political and religious ideologies are especially destructive because of their authority and power.

Youth is enthused by ideals. Youth demands to know the sense and purpose of life, and expects an answer in authoritative expression, which demonstrates how life is to be shaped.

Those who were once followers of supposed "ideals" and who felt keen disappointment in upholding such concepts (e.g. many supporters of Nazism, Communism, or other political or religious ideologies) have since tossed these so-called ideals overboard, together with their idealism, and now regard themselves to yet *another* ideology. To have ideals and to be an idealist assumes an aura of naivete in such instances. These disappointed individuals, however, never became conscious of their pursuit of an ideology, or realized that the labored under a false ideal.

Exactitude of Psychologic Norm

Whoever has learned to think critically will demand that any assertion be proven with irrefutable logic. Ideal-norms are never to be accepted in good faith, whether of a religious, political, or scientific ideology.

With the aid of functional psychology, psychological norms may be fixed logically, precisely, and scientifically.

Functional psychology is a four-dimensional system based on a mathematical methodology, and is therefore an exact, logical system in which systematic relations become provable, and are in tune with reality.

Similar to the application of mathematics to astronomy or to the periodic tables of chemistry, the functional-psychologic system can be employed to predict psychologic conduct, even before it occurs. Subsequently, statistical proof will confirm the scientific exactness of the functional psychologic basis.

Functional Psychology

Functional psychology defines and explains the relation between subject and object.

Every subject assumes a position in this relationship. This position (place, situation, direction, order) is the first necessary distinction out of four:

I. Position: functional psychology differentiates in the first dimension between two opposing positions (similar to masculine/ feminine, will/feeling, animus/anima, parental "me"/ infantile "me").

The two possible positions are:

Autonomous: the subject determines, or influences the object or partner (e.g. authoritatively)

Heteronomous: the subject permits itself to be determined or influenced by the object or partner (e.g. in good faith).

II. Direction: the second necessary distinction is the subject's direction vis-à-vis the object. Functional psychology differentiates two possible directions of a relationship (similar to C.G. Jung's "Introversion-Extroversion"). *Concentric* object (e.g. the specific partner, "external world") directed toward a constant "me-inner world," a specific target of the *Excentric* objects e.g. partners, directed toward changing environment, changing situations).

III. Change of direction: position and direction combine to shape relations. Position or direction can change in two possible movements:

attraction (+): affirmation, sympathy
aversion (−): denial, antipathy.

IV. Speed of change: if movement is not uniform
or constant but changeable. This fourth
dimension is especially important in the
psychology of conflict. An accelerated attachment is recognized as a compulsive addiction,
e.g., to alcoholism, tobacco or drug dependency (or at least as a torturous yearning).
Similarly, the accelerated motion is recognized as a phobia, such as the fear when an
expected partner doesn't show up at the
appointed hour, or is absent without calling,
or even if menstruation doesn't occur on
schedule. Functional psychology thus distinguishes as the fourth dimension:

"Compulsion: accelerated attachment,
yearning, "neurotic" needs, compensations,
urgently required."

Fear: accelerated aversion, slowing down,
inhibition, repression, neurotic inhibition
of needs, avoidance at any cost. (In the
color test, this appears as an empty column and demonstrates psychosomatic sen-
sitizing).

The first and second dimension, position and
direction, never occur in isolation, but always in
combination (autonomous or heteronomous) with a

direction (concentric or excentric). We therefore see four basic structures:

	Heteronomous	Autonomous
EXCENTRIC	different adventure solution change distance yellow	to dominate others excitement activity sufficiency of allure red
CONCENTRIC	*Experiencing oneself* rest satisfaction void of allure blue	*Conquering oneself* tension persistence narrowness green

Other foursomes represent numerous well-known, functional systems: the four directions of the compass, the four elements (fire, water, air, earth), the four basic colors (blue, green, red, yellow), the four temperaments, the four personality "types" of C.G. Jung, Erich Fromm, V.E. Frankl, and Sigmund Freud (although Freud omitted the fourth erotic direction) oral, anal, genital, visual.

Both dimensions—direction and position—are capable of being depicted as a square:

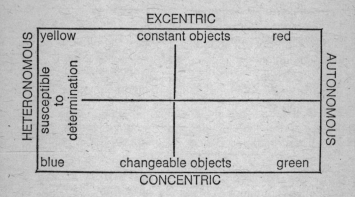

This logical system, related to medical-physiological and psychological reality, means:

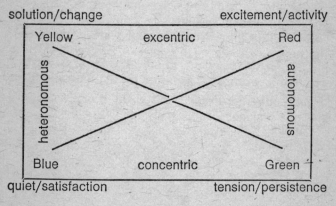

The four logical structures have the following meaning in the realm of self-estimation; they are designated as the four "ego norms":

Structure and Meaning	Ego Norm
excentric-heteronomous (yellow): use of given possibilities, free and independent	independent development of the self
excentric-autonomous (red): strength and achievement potential, actively utilized	self-confidence
concentric-heteronomous (blue): acquiescing to a given situation	modesty
concentric-autonomous (green): acting according to one's own conviction, identity	self-esteem

These four normal, self-assessments (me-norms) are combined in pairs to the six normal me-structures (personality structures):

Combination of the four me-norms:	Me-structures:
self-esteem and self-development	= independence

self-esteem and self-confidence	= self-assurance
self-esteem and self-determination	= seriousness
self-confidence and self-development	= cheerfulness
self-confidence and self-determination	= contentment
self-determination and self-development	= untroubled unconcern

The me-norms (normal self-assessment) of functional psychology:

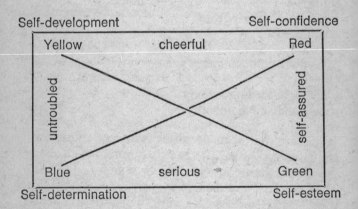

The basic social norms thus derive from the systematic and precise analysis of the me-norms. Thus a logical and psychologically exact ethic replaces an empirical and religious hypothetical ethic.

There is a substantial parallel with Judeo-Christian commandments: *sincerity:* Thou shalt not bear false witness; *honesty:* Thou shalt not steal; *tolerance:* Thou shalt not kill; *benevolence:* Honor thy father and mother. Yet our logically derived basic norms are not defensive commandments (thou shalt not . . .) and it is particularly pleasing that in addition to fostering benevolence and loving kindness they proclaim, as a kind of moral commandment, the necessity of open-mindedness as well. Until now, we found lack of interest and absence of enthusiasm to be vexatious and bothersome, but we cannot regard them as moral failure or as an offense against the basic norm of open-mindedness.

These ideal-norms (the me-norms as well as social norms) are no moralizing commandments, nor are they ideologies one-sidedly based on a specific ideal. The ideal-norms are orientation aids; they indicate direction like signposts on the way to self-realization. Ideals are basic direction indicators which are not acquired at birth or through theoretical lore.

The target to which ideals point is normalcy. That target is tantamount to self-realization, which is an art that must be learned like every art; it must be practiced and implemented. Its targets, normalcy and naturalness, guarantee an optimal mode of living.

Self-deception

The individual, that creature who constantly asks "Who am I?" can easily depart from the direct route to healthy, normal conduct (denoted by the symbol "="). He may establish absolute demands (symbolized by "+"), or he assumes an unconditionally defensive posture (whose symbol is "−").

The realm of calm (demand)
The demanding posture

An exaggerated demand cannot relate to the real world around us, but becomes an absolute demand (+): "I want, under any circumstances...." It makes no difference whether the demand asks for unconditional love, or is a full-blown delusion of grandeur: "I determine the fate of the next thousand years." (Hitler)

Impending fear

Every absolute demand ("I demand that you regard me as sympathetic") creates fear ("Under no circumstances am I to be deemed unsympathetic"). Every absolute demand (+) immediately induces fear, albeit subconsciously, because we know deep inside that we've exceeded reality. This impeding fear ("No, under no circumstances!") appears as a defensive posture, and we denote it with "−".

Each + (demand) produces a − (fear), and the converse is true as well: the bigger the fear, the more pressure to realize the demand.

I call this balance between excessive demand

(+) and fear (−) "function." Function in mathematics denotes the dependence of one entity upon another; the rise of one side of a scale is directly related to the descent of the opposite side.

In our example, the descending side of the scale represents inhibiting fear and feelings of inferiority. The ascending side of the scale corresponds to excessive demands and the exaggerated urge to appear important. Both sides constantly manifest themselves in the same individual.

The pivot, the fixed point at which the scale is suspended, is the knowledge of reality—conviction or conscience.

There is a functional dependence between excessive and absolute demand (+) and fear (−). For example, the balance between aggressiveness and helplessness, between yearning for contact and fear of isolation, or the struggle between a person's hard core and his softer side. The same concept is characterized by the expression "ambivalence," if it is employed in its proper psychologic sense.

The Me-Realm
The Me-Idol

Each absolute demand alters one's self-reliance. Because I demand unconditionally that my personal request must be fulfilled (e.g. to be called the foremost physician, or to be *simpatico* in everyone's eyes) I am developing an overvalued, illusory, and overestimated self-assuredness. We'll symbolize this with the term "me-idol" (+). Now my self-assuredness depends on the degree to which my absolute demands are being met.

The Me-Fear

Every unconditional demand contains some apprehension: "Under no circumstances do I want that ... I fear that. ..." That apprehension can cause inhibiting fear, which alters my self-reliance. Thus undervalued, illusory self-reliance we shall call "me-fear."

Behavior in the Environment
Conduct of the Idol-Role

The absolute demands of the me-idol will necessarily alter our conduct vis-à-vis the environment.

The me-idol, the illusion that I play a starring role professionally or socially, demands not only that I act the part, but requires that I assume corresponding attributes as well: house, car, etc. Without a choice in the matter, without reference to reality, I now do everything I assume this idol-role demands of me. My behavior is no longer determined by external reality; it now springs from inner apprehension, the me-fear. I no longer select my car according to my needs, but according to the status of my idol role.

The choice of an idol-car, as much as all other compensating conduct, is in fact a signal. It says: "Look at my car; it'll tell you who I am." When car, title, house, wealth, etc., primarily serve as prestige-signals toward self-assertion, the relationship to reality is lost.

Conduct in the Defensive-Role

Exorbitant, indiscriminate demands (+) are found in functional interdependence with repression

$(-)$; forming the defensive posture of indecision. The defensive-role manifests itself as indifference, prejudice, unobjective criticism, or animosity. It also results in conduct unrelated to reality: indolence, inhibition, compulsion, depression, phobia, and even destructiveness,

Such destructive, hostile conduct must be recognized as a symbol of subconscious fear of living. Fear of life does not only manifest itself in aggression, but in regression as well, e.g. in such phrases as "What will be, will be. . . . there's nothing we can do about it" or in extreme sensitivity or irritability, in humble mockery, and spiteful derision.

Defensive conduct may also become evident through indifference of the heart and indolence of mind. The individual who relates to reality will always react spontaneously—whether happy or concerned. Absence of these normal reactions are an alarm signal.

The countless signals which we employ to convince others of our idol-role are explained in the table that follows.

Many play the idol-role of the "decent" person by forcing their sexuality into a defensive-role; they calculate their sensuality (Freud identifies the defensive-role, the "id" with the sexual urge). Many young people today regard sexiness as a personification of the idol-role, the "super-me." Conversely, a person's mental abilities are relegated to the defensive role, the "id." Cultural values of the older generation are viewed with contempt.

Chapter 2

Role-Playing Signals and Status Symbols

These days, a role can be any activity or social position. But if you extend the concept of "role" to include each function and every "slotting" into social strata, then this term becomes a mere fashionable expression without any deeper meaning.

This kind of popularizing of the word would attach a host of different interpretations to it, as for example if you were to refer to the role of a mother. Thus, when a woman becomes a mother, she'll have:

1. another activity, or function
2. a different insight into herself
3. a different social position.

If a mother says to her child: "I have brought you a doll," she speaks in the function of the mother. But if she says, "Look at what Mommy brought you," she holds a mirror to herself and plays the *role* of mother. Therefore, to accurately define the concept of "role," I will limit the definition to self-portrayal. Then self-reliance determines—as would a stage manager—the role one would play and the requisites one would use: dress, home furnishings, and the like. R. Linton has defined "status," clearly and accurately, all those duties and rights a person has in society. The shepherd has his status, just as the president does. Relatively speaking, status symbols change their meaning. They are symbols of duties and rights according to one's position in society. One recognizes the uniform of a policeman or a custom agent as a status symbol, just as one regards the physician's white coat, a nun's habit, the license plate of a diplomat's car, a king's crown, the top hat of a European chimney sweep, and a chef's tall hat. A title such as M.D., or a professional label such as minister or reverend, are status characteristics. The say nothing about the person's self-esteem.

A nun may have more guilt feelings than a prostitute; the chimney sweep may wear his top hat with more pride than a king his crown. If we take the sociologic definition of the status concept seriously, then neither a Rolls Royce nor the emblem of the Rotary Club is a genuine status symbol. Neither the villa with a swimming pool and servants, nor a mink coat, nor going to church on Sunday denote genuine status, i.e., function in society.

In most cases, however, these are full-grown

role-signals; they don't reveal duties or rights, but they do tell us much about the illusory self-esteem of the person.

I would like to limit my discussion of self-esteem to its relationship with the environment. To me, then, the word "role" means neither position in society, status (such as that of physician or mother), or function, but solely and exclusively the judgment of one's own person—how I think the environment judges me. It helps me to know what I represent to a specific individual, for instance a lover, a marriage partner, a son, a business partner, or a segment of society (i.e., one's own family, the nation, or all of humanity). The word "role" thus means to me the illusion of my own self-judgment, and my resulting attitude and conduct.

We must realize that our illusionary and fictitious self-judgment and self-esteem dictates our conduct; despite our real accomplishments, we play a role.

Playing a role reaches a psychopathologic level in hysterical sickness, with accompanying psychosomatic symptoms. Illusionary self-reliance always determines whether or not we play a role, and the kind of role we play relative to society. Prerequisite to role-playing is a self-esteem which has degenerated into self-judgment (I am stupid or intelligent, good-looking or unattractive, insignificant or influential).

The extraordinary yoga lessons of Satipatthana and the teaching of Socrates ("I know that I know nothing") represent a sense of the self which intends to protect man against infantile self-judgments that may have grave consequences. Occidental cultures were unable to lead people to this self-conscious humility. Hence our I-mania leads us from self-admiration to frequently subconscious self-contempt, from the superego to the impersonal "id," from heaven to hell. Preoccupation with the self can be a barrier against reality, hurting self-preservation with its egocentric self-delusion, denying us the "healthier egotism."

In an egocentric desire to be something or somebody, we are tempted to play the role of hero and ultimately sacrifice property and life.

Genuine self-esteem and self-judgment eliminates self-overevaluating. It avoids self-illusion, which can result in I-the-idol on the one hand, and self-fright or a self-defensive role on the other. Self-illusion keeps us from reality, and thus from self-realization.

If we're to interpret self-confidence and self-reliance properly, it becomes the opposite of reality. Self-esteem and self-realization become opponents of our environment.

Both provinces, then, the illusionary self-esteem as well as the relationship to the environment, become contradictory. Our illusionary self-esteem splits into "I-the-idol" dreams (for example, the desire to live a carefree and comfortable existence) and the secret "frightened self" (inner distress over tasks at hand and fear of failure in life).

The relationship to the environment splits into polarized behavior patterns; on the one hand, the role of the idol, the programmed target one strains to achieve, on the other hand, the defensive-role which causes us to avoid certain situations at all costs.

Because we fear inherent danger, it is a situation we fight on all kinds of pretext.

We express our apprehension: "I should say not!" or "I can't afford that," "I have no time to indulge in such pleasures," at the same time as we express our target program: "I want to assert myself and achieve a measure of success."

Extensive psychodiagnostic examinations (especially the clinical color test and combined form-and-color test used in psychosomatic medicine) have shown that artificially graded self-esteem influences the individual's conduct vis-à-vis his environment. This interdependence has been known for a long time as the tough exterior (the role) vs. the soft core (the "I"). We know that people with tact, charm, and diplomacy also play a role, and play it well; mostly they pursue their goals with determined consistency and impervious self-assertion.

EXAMPLE:

A "I-the-IDOL" (influences a)
"I need a partner who loves me absolutely and without any conditions."

a DEFENSIVE-ROLE (influences A
"I guard against showing my love if I can't be absolutely sure that I'm being unconditionally loved."

B "The FEAR-I" (influences b)
"I have a secret fear of loneliness and isolation."

b IDOL-ROLE (influences B)
"I seek contact with people who appreciate and love me."

37

BASIC TYPES OF FUNCTIONAL PSYCHOLOGY

	Blue	Green	Red	Yellow
"I-Self-consciousness"		Conduct vis-à-vis environment		
		Idol-role (+) "Target" (Urge toward)		
I-the-idol (+) (Excessive self- consciousness)				
	+1	+2	+3	+4
Pretension: absolute (I must have at all costs)	satisfaction stupefaction regression	authority impressing positions of prestige	to experience excitability irritability	independence search escape from problem

Self-Unconsciousness (==) Pretension: relative (I would like)	Self-Realization			
	=1 tranquility relaxation satisfaction	=2 firmness persistence automatic navigating	=3 excitement motion activity	=4 solution change unfolding
The Fear-I (—) Pretension: absolutely not (I don't want under any circumstances)	Defensive Role (—) "Warding-Off" (scared of . . .)			
	—1 attraction-void boredom love-privation	—2 narrowness dependence duress	—3 excessive attraction satiety exhaustion	—4 expanse loss forlorn

My concept of "type" always denotes a specific behavior pattern, never the nature or character of the individual. "Type" therefore means only a dominant pattern. One and the same person may be a "Red Type" sexually, but a "Green Type" in the choice of his home furnishings.

The Defensive Role of the "Blue Type" (—Blue)
Fear of Emptiness and Deprivation

Obviously, there are individuals and situations which can bore you to death. But whoever is dissatisfied because of his own passiveness ("It doesn't pay" or "There's no sense to it") or because of demands which cannot be realized, generates his own fear of getting the short end of a deal. It's a fear of having to sacrifice something you may need for personal contentment. The fear of this "happening-void" produces an inner unrest or agitation. The fear of being frustrated makes the subject shun an unsatisfactory relationship or job situation.

If, as it often happens, inner aversion or distrust persists because a commitment cannot be resolved, the relationship or situation cools. At best, it flickers into a low flame of indifference. The suppressed dissatisfaction in such a reciprocal arrangement is rarely expressed in direct language.

Instead apprehension grows. The liaison may evolve into an unsatisfying void, blocking a genuine relationship, and preventing confidence in a reciprocal, sensible understanding and a bond of feeling and emotion.

As a matter of self-protection, many people fence in their emotions, permitting a partner to approach only by degrees. We subtly measure safe distances on a case-by-case basis. Within each "case," the partner may use his own discretion in approaching. We may consciously regulate contact-attitudes by failing to greet someone, or being brusque or polite, in a social situation. We can act gentle, emotional, orgasm-prone, intimately sincere, and confidential in a love relationship, or criticize our partner with a perfunctory peck on the cheek instead of a kiss on the lips.

When the "giving of self" is blocked, emotions are dammed up. ("What's going on with him?" "What's he thinking now?") Since these feelings are not based on reality, they're replaced by an imaginary and unreal relationship. We're apt to use clichés in place of actual communication: "What's your zodiac sign?"

Whenever emotions or feelings are blocked by fear, reality and meaningful experiences are replaced by irrationality, superstition, and sometimes even hallucinations. In this secret, introverted jungle of emotions, sentimental or heroic daydreams may flourish.

The Idol-Role of the "Blue Type" (+Blue)
The Regressive Urge for Satisfaction

Contentment (—Blue) may be so totally absent that we develop a pressing need for anything that brings satisfaction, quiet, and relaxation. A forgetful stupor is the target of this urge (+Blue): either through physical anesthesia such as excessive sexuality, gluttony, alcoholism, tranquilizers, and sedatives, or by reducing demands on our mentality (e.g. solving an easier crossword puzzle). Regression is a preferred escape route, a backward step to a carefree satisfaction of bodily functions. Another is restoring to the "simple life," the uninhibited natural state of the child. Females may take flight into childbearing, thus seeking escape from occupational or marital difficulties.

Managerial individuals under stress may flee back to nature by buying a farm or designing a rustic den or bar for the house.

The Defensive Role of the "Green Type"
(—Green)
Fear of Narrowness, Dependence and Duress

Duress needn't be a forceful threat from without. The pressure to buy an ostentatious alligator handbag originates neither from the alligator nor from the handbag. Even if we must eat to satisfy our hunger, it does not constitute duress, but rather a necessity. When it comes to necessities, the "must" ought to be a desire. Need must not be misinterpreted as arbitrary compulsion. Whoever wants to buy must also pay. Whoever makes demands must also count on refusals. We must be prepared to do something in return. This constitutes real necessity and self-discipline, realistic self-direction (=green): "I decide what I want and what I'm prepared to pay for it. The course I choose determines in advance that I'm capable of demanding, as well as of doing without."

Whoever makes absolute demands cannot renounce or do without. That person is not prepared to render payment. Thus he becomes prisoner of his own demands. He resembles the monkey who gets caught because he won't let go of the banana he wants to pull through the narrow neck of a bottle.

Whoever makes excessive demands without concessions in return, whoever wants to be admired and beloved by one and all, or who demands blind obedience, simply ignores the give-and-take of reality. He is incapable of returning an accommodation, a favor, a service. He cannot admire people, or love them, or permit them to age gracefully. Because he makes total and unequivocal demands, he perceives reality as restriction and duress. He invents "white lies" to escape its necessities.

Evasion by subterfuge and excuse becomes a mode of living, and eventually "the big lie" destroys self-confidence. Because we don't want to make any sacrifices, we diminish our decisiveness, our ability to make *any* decisions. We feel dependent and wind up in a dead end. Our assumed dependence (for example, that of a wife) is seen as an insurmountable obstacle. It makes a sensible self-realization impossible. But it is the only demand that requires no concessions and makes "doing without" most difficult. Because we want both—possession and availability, as well as independence and freedom—we're unable to make *any* decision. This may lead to a block against initiative of any kind, so we make the best of

43

any situation. We find ourselves living in an apparent readiness to compromise.

The Idol Role of the "Green Type" (+Green)
The Urge to Impress

Insecurity is an intolerable state. Everything that guarantees security, solidity, persistence, and durability is supposedly qualified to banish one's own insecurity.

Everything we acquire and call our own should confirm to the bystander (and ourselves) that we're at least that which we possess; if we represent the value of our possessions. That is a fallacy. Possession has questionable value to self-assertion, and does not represent a sound basis for self-confidence.

Self-assertion—as opposed to self-confidence—uses many forms of self-possession, preferably a material solidity. This can range from solid physical girth to "solid" wealth. Self-assertion can also find expression in ideologies adopted to impress oneself and others with the "idol role."

Chances of success depend less on special abilities than on the clever appearance of a decisive role and knowing what one's contacts appreciate: politically popular opinions, moral hypocrisy, or obscene literature.

Acceptance is everything; influence and value at any price, even at the risk of total exposure. Every attempt to impress others—by fashionable dress or flashy sports car—is bound to generate a lasting effect.

But if we think in terms of long-range goals vs.

short-term advantages, we may prefer to play that "impressive role" on a far more solid base.

Striving for a position of prestige which will help maintain a permanent impression. Academic titles, for instance, secure a lifetime of prestige, whereas titles of nobility endure beyond a generation. Owning your home and furnishings will impress new visitors, and thus insure continuing prestige. Automobiles and neckties, by contrast, are only impressive as long as they are new and useful.

It is far less expensive to place your pride in performing duties with modesty and morality. Stubborn principles, moralistic or political pronouncements, fashionable scientific opinions, religious dogmas, and intolerance are actually "roles created to impress," and are *all* frequently classed as intolerance.

Behind such masks we find a stubborn know-it-all, a pedant, an "I-cripple" hiding his hunger for power. Similarly enduring are people with a penchant for proverbs, truisms, and "bedside philosophy," who try to impress us with modest words ("I merely think . . .") and offering empty advice.

Though some use their urge to dominate to reach greatness—as a general in the army—another may try to dominate his children or his spouse. This urge may turn into manipulation ("I can't sleep if you aren't at home yet.").

But if an individual "impression-role" won't suffice because of our feeling of inferiority, we resort to a higher, even more different type of "order." We identify with an ideological principle or group. The ugly caterpillar of individual ego develops into a splendid butterfly by submerging itself in the powerful "we" of group identity.

"We academicians," "we pedestrians," "we young boys," "we men." Instead of the more personal "You just wont grant my wishes," a wife can now use the "we" of sexuality and accuses her mate thus: "You just don't understand us women."

The "Green Type" is the most intense, persistent, stable, and immune to outside influence. This makes it difficult to shed the role of self-assertiveness and to return to the more realistic role of self-realization.

Defensive Role of the "Red Type"
(—Red) *Fear of Challenge and Overchallenge*

Excitement that spawns reluctance, becomes annoyance. If it's more intense, we call it anger, and when it is aimless and purposeless, we call it rage. But if it persists, it can disgust and sicken us. Why? Simply because these manifestations run counter to our intentions.

General McAuliffe's famous expletive "Nuts!" and the more modern "Up yours!" are expressions of anger or rage. They signify a situation in which "We've had it up to here!"—"We could puke!" to use a more aggravated expression. Things that are too much for us and cause us to burst are readily equated with parts of the body or with bodily function. The more erudite scientists—psychiatrists, for example—use the learned and euphemistic declaration that we experience "excessive demands on our capacity to cope with certain occurrences."

If our essential wants seem endangered, an overchallenge results (—Red). The excessive challenge produces anger (Such a mean trick!") when the discrimination or handicap is seen to devalue our self-reliance (—Green).

The overchallenge becomes defiance ("I simply won't stand for that!") the moment we defend ourselves with a self-glorifying desire to show off (+Green) against this deflating influence.

If we try to ignore a conflict, the overchallenge cannot unfold. It does, however, cause psychologically induced fatigue, and can lead to exhaustion and depression. The urge to escape problems, the desire to relieve ourselves of a burden, comes out in common or trivial gestures such as waving the hand as if to push something away, stroking the hair, scratching the scalp, or humming or whistling.

The excessive challenge (—Red) leads to a reluctant or inhibited depression. This happens when urgent needs seem unsatisfied, either now and forever, or when we are forced to recognize our powerlessness, and seek to anesthetize ourselves through sleep or alcohol.

The onset of such overchallenge may be recognized by a feeling of reluctance. This symptom is diagnosed as "irritating weakness" or "neurasthenia."

The Idol-Role of the "Red Type" (+Red)
The Mania of Challenge or Attraction

To live well, and to function as well as a military trainee at target practice, does not constitute living as we humans deserve it. Even if we immerse ourselves in champagne and caviar, or if we hold an exalted position, we are not living life to the fullest. Unless these subtle sensations are perceived by a vibrant consciousness and become part of our way of living, our life remains a mere existence, insensible functioning, or vegetating.

Suppose you pack yourself full of foreign language lessons, art history, and adult education courses, all designed to occupy your meaningless existence. You might be hiding instead of "living."

To be human in the sense of being a fulfilled human being is to experience as much of the world as our consciousness and intensity will let us absorb. We thus *seek* the challenge of living.

However, in turning toward life, we may play the idol-role, engaging in a frantic search for dares and challenges, especially if we use it to compensate for a phobia of even a mild apprehension.

Three different fear-motives are expressed in as many diverse manifestations of compulsive search for challenge. Fear of void and boredom (—Blue) leads to a challenge-mania (+Red) and manifests itself as stimulation urge. The void in an emotional relationship, missing sympathy, a lack of congeniality—they all need to be replaced by some kind of attraction. The danger becomes using intimate situations as stimuli. This supposed intimacy may erupt in quasi-psychologic care of a companion, or in a *contretemps* in a bar or in the bedroom.

A yearning for challenge can spring from fear of inferiority. By pressuring ourselves to be assertive or to seek the limelight of attention, we submit to an enduring compulsion.

Compulsive types won't emerge voluntarily from

this state of tension. Rather, they will attempt to resolve their quandary through further challenges. Since that requires a steady stream of *new* challenge situations, a compulsive individual is forever forced into activity. His curse is the vigorous urge for any undertaking or enterprise. His achievements may be minor or significant; they may benefit or injure his fellow humans.

We may manifest self-imposed pressure in brawling or by forcing ourselves to athletic achievements of Olympic dimensions—perhaps to reach international renown.

The third fear is the phobia of becoming isolated (—Yellow). Whoever imagines himself to be a grain of sand on the wide seashore of life sees his insignificance compared to world events. The hopelessness of being lost or isolated may induce a panicked fear, and thereby cause flight into a challenge situation. If you are afraid in a dark forest, you might start to sing at the top of your lungs. If that feeling crops up in your home, you may turn up your stereo fullblast, and thus flood your consciousness with a "challenge."

Fear of isolation is strong enough to force us to hide in something that occupies our senses.

We become "insanely" interested, totally possessed. We occupy ourselves, body and soul, afire with inspiration and enthusiasm. We laugh insanely, for example.

We fill the frightening expanse of our inner loneliness with stimulating challenges (+Red). This obsessive urge is an attempt to save ourselves from aimlessness and emptiness.

If that urge survives beyond our youth, the quest for challenges makes us seek a more important target. We find it among those who do more than vegetate or merely function. We find it in cultured surroundings, in *joie de vivre*. Our three virtues are enjoyment, wealth, and independence.

The person with a petty or small mentality whose phobias make him seek challenges at a lower level sees these virtues in his own way: sex, money, and opposition, or anarchy. His enjoyment remains a listless function. This type of small-minded *bon vivant* is justly referred to as a playboy.

The Defensive-Role of the "Yellow Type"
(*—Yellow*) *Fear of Distance, Expanse, Loss*

The frequent fear of loss is a theme of countless variations of the "Yellow Type"; the fear of losing whatever security, renown, or self-assurance we have. The environment is forever changing, and thereby altering our own position.

Whoever doesn't adjust to these ever-changing situations and does not apply himself realistically, pragmatically realizing *himself*, must then live in fear of such changes. Fear of the immensity of such endless possibilities is frequently linked with fear of a hugh container, a mammoth room, or even an immense open space—agoraphobia. That person considers himself lost.

Constant changes in reality, changing developments in one's occupation or profession, perhaps, growing older, or change in one's economic situation must not be ignored by restoring to the defensive-role of self-consciousness. Constant change must be countered by an ongoing adjustment.

"Hope" is the traditional name for the acceptance of change. When hope (+Yellow) derives from a pragmatically measured conviction ("I hope it'll succeed"), we possess the power of faith that can "move mountains."

Realistic hope is the antithesis of self-illusion, the "hope of faith." Illusion is the pitiless diagnosis for all those pinning their hopes on good fortune in the hereafter. Someone who seeks and finds his fortune in a *worldly* paradise surrenders unrealistic aspirations of a heavenly reward.

On the opposite side, we find an individual who views reality as a vale of sorrows surrounded by a mirage of paradise. His idea of heaven is peopled by old-fashioned saints and newfangled idols. He sees life as a search for safety, as if it were an overstuffed easy chair or a burglar-proof safe. That individual will be disillusioned, either by degrees or all at once. Then he'll pretend life has cheated him, finding reality unfathomable and treacherous. He feels threatened by it. This widespread fear is commonly accepted as a "need for security."

These dwarflike martyrs who've been "disappointed by life" are stuck fast on the glue of safety. Conservative society accepts them as long as they "play it cool and conventional." According to either religious or secular jargon, they call their crutches celibacy, poverty, and obedience, or decency, altruism, and industrious performance of their duties. If you pursue these virtues to the end of your days, society will reward you with a huge obituary notice.

Chronic sacrifice will be rewarded by a splendid eulogy.

The sensation of being lost is familiar to many through its harmless first stage, the distance between themselves and their fellow creatures. The inability to relate settles like a gentle autumn haze over family and friends, until they disappear altogether in an ever-thickening fog. Their speech reaches you as if through a muffled duct. The loss of relationship and inner distance makes you feel like a spectator to an event onstage.

The feeling of remoteness may grow ever further, to a sensation of limitless expanse and aloneness, to a point where there's neither end, nor safety, nor security. There comes an aura of helplessness, of being lost in the universe. This fear of diminished importance (−Yellow) and the drive to impress (+Green) are permanently fused together. The need for security is then called "self-assertion" and becomes the ideal "personality corset."

This urge for self-confirmation, this ceremonial dance around the golden calf, needs an audience, though perhaps only an imaginary one. But such an urge frequently becomes a desire to show off, to assert your validity.

The continuing tension brought about by the need for security, the urge to assert yourself, and the pressure to validate your existence can lead to psychosomatic spasms of the smooth muscle. Examples of their manifestation would be spasms of the stomach, of the gall bladder, or of the intestines. Migraines may result. Feelings of excessive irritation

or excitement are another effect of constant inner
tension caused by self-imposed pressure. This irritating obsession spreads like wildfire fanned by the self-
assertion urge. Malevolence, anger, and aggressiveness are unleashed ("I'll show that guy a thing or
two!").

Based solely on psychologic definition, every
form of aggression is motivated by fear-induced self-
assertiveness. Aggression presupposes "neurotic" self-
assertiveness, a compensation for fear. Any act
dictated by vital necessity, such as an animal's hunt
for prey, therefore cannot be equated with aggression.

When we appear forlorn because we lost a
partner (—Yellow) and are at the same time afraid
of the impending void and deprivation (—Blue),
both manifestations combine into a common dread
of loneliness.

Against this unfortunate combination of sensations, a sense of pride comes into play. The fear of
loneliness and hurt pride together sire a new feeling
—jealousy. This burdensome sensation of tension
now quickly leads to excitement.

The thunderstorm begins to unleash, agrressive
jealousy comes into the open, and not one piece of
china or genuine partnership is safe. Fear of loneliness, of loss of relationship and isolation (—Yellow)
may, as statistics confirm, release alcoholism and drug
addiction.

Many adults suck habitually on the pacifier of
alcohol, or seek satisfaction by deep drafts on a cigar,
pipe, or cigarette. They cling to their "cherished

habits" like a child to his mother's apron strings. The self-assured adult really doesn't know what to do with the safety so vital to an insecure baby.

The need to be rocked in the sheltered cradle, or to hide behind an adult "pacifier," results from fear of insecurity and loneliness (—Yellow) coupled with the urge for satisfaction (+Blue). The sentimental urge to "cling," the infantile need of shelter, impairs every sensible and meaningful partnership, because a genuine adult relationship is based on an internal independence, a feeling of safety and security.

The Idol-Role of the "Yellow Type"
The Urge for Liberty or Liberation

There are individuals who torture themselves every weekend with a frantic search for a distant goal. There are many who use up their vacation time, year after year, in search of something unknown, unique, and novel. Some don't travel at all—they become "armchair travellers," immersed in a world of travel brochures.

It isn't the spatial target that attracts, but the urge to reach the unknown, the quest for change, the greed for something new, or just plain curiosity. The mill runs, the waterwheel turns, even if there's no grist to grind. The drive of such individuals is manifest as a yearning for change in many ways, from "wanderlust" to a life as a vagabond, from extramarital adventure to national migration, from decorating a home to world revolution.

Children in our progressive day and age view

the concepts of "new" and "modern" as tree ornaments at Christmas time. The word "future" becomes
their treetop ornament. They expect paradise on
earth in the future, and the solution to all their problems. The quest for change and their curiosity as to
what the future may hold represents a flight from
the present because reality seems unsatisfactory,
empty and boring (—Blue).

The urge to liberate ourselves from a paralyzing
and depressing dependence, to save ourselves from
being sucked into a state of depression, produces an
inner unrest and drive. It is the most frequent reason
that we seek freedom (+Yellow). Together they
result in an urge to "cast off." Statistics prove that
this compulsion forms a common personality structure.

While depression is shunted aside, it remains in
our subconscious ("masked depression"). Our physical well-being is affected, and we react with psychosomatic complaints. Once the urge to "be rid of," to
"cast ourselves loose," results in acute illness, the
result will be a clinical diagnosis of "agitated psychotic depression." The urge to be liberated (+Yel-
low) and the unbridled yearning to be rid of the
shackles of complaints, duress, and constriction
(—Green), combine to form a yearning for independence.

Whoever feels hemmed in by his parental home,
an authoritarian partner, or his external situation in
life, or whoever imposes some kind of pressure on
himself, feels the urge to break out of such a situation. He experiences a strong desire to be free. He
wants to escape the cage of his own demands, or the

obligations which constrict him. He wants to travel far, to fly away, to find new contacts, establish interesting relationships. These are the vivid and spirited expectations of those with a compulsion to be free. Whoever is imprisoned by his urge to be something or somebody needs to be set free. He makes himself the hero of the drive to freedom. With the battle cry of "Emancipation!" he labels himself a "heck of a guy."

Safety and impressiveness, the sandbags which conservative and older generations use as ballast, are his adversaries.

The excessive challenge (—Red) may quickly lead in anger to "hitting the ceiling," sputtering and fuming, and a compelling urge to get rid of the vexation, perhaps verbally—hence the army slogan "Curse aloud to free yourself!"

Chapter 3

Signals of Dress

"Clothes make the man" really means "like dress, like personality." Appearance and being are as close to each other as are clothes to one's skin. An illegally worn officer's tunic made a poor soul into the famous "Captain of Köpenick" (the role so deliciously parodied several decades ago by Danny Kaye). Conversely, Andersen's charming fairy tale, "The Emperor's New Clothes," shows a personality creating an outward illusion through dress. The undressed emperor couldn't be seen in the altogether— hence, the people imagined seeing their monarch in resplendent garments.

There are clothes whose function is to protect against colds and draft, like long underwear. Then there are clothes whose purpose is to hide; beneath the showy hat lies a bald pate. Finally, we find garments that are meant to *show* what they cover. The most ancient example of this is the "clerically tailored" fig leaf. Later, the miniskirt, barely a hand's width wider, was more popular proof of this phenomenon.

Whether fig leaf or crinoline, short or long, whatever is worn as fashionable dress is pure convention and cannot be charged to the wearer's personality.

Whether a man is smooth-shaven or grows a "personality beard," whether he wears straight or flared slacks, none of these represents a personality symbol. Fashion, no matter how unusual, conspicuous, or shocking it may be, is never a key to man's personality. It is a style, and nothing more.

By his style we're apt to recognize the senior clerk, the worker, the director, the cleaning woman, the actress, or the left-wing intellectual. Almost subconsciously, people select their clothes from available styles to correspond best to the role they want to assume.

Dress in such cases is a disguise. Wrapping the body in fabrics creates the role-image. The fabric shell is meant to upgrade the net content. There are inconsiderate business people who, because of their profit hunger and greed we could imagine as unshaven and barefoot clods dressed in buffalo skin. In reality, they don't look like guerrilla fighters or big game hunters at all; they dress unobtrusively and in a refined manner.

If we gear our functionally psychological views

to the world of textiles, the shell becomes transparent; personality constants become fully visible.

Dress as Idol-Role and Defensive-Role

Some people intentionally—albeit subconsciously—select clothes that conform to an image, an example. Their pattern may be a specific person: a friend, a revered teacher, a political idol, or a social group. The idol-role demands serious conventional dress (almost like a store window mannequin), and this defensive-role forbids this person to remove his jacket, even at the height of summer, even if a heat stroke were to transform him into a well-clad corpse. The idol-role of the revolutionary demands that he open his shirt collar wide enough to expose his heroic chest, and *his* defensive role keeps him from wearing a bourgeois necktie even in a Siberian cold wave.

A stylish, dashing female believes she must top current fashion with her own extravagance, while the seedy moralist is content to look as dull and plain as a dust cloth. The classic strength which suits serious Papa smells musty to his smart, racy daughter.

The self-sufficient and independent miss will want to prove that a sense of duty and moral narrowness don't satisfy her. She'll telegraph those sentiments with a provocatively short or long skirt, or by some other inciting manner of dress. Extravagance doesn't necessarily have to provoke by overt sex; she may portray the same female sass or arrogance by wearing an unusual hat. Extravagance is forever signified by an increasing demand to show off. That, in turn, derives from the feeling that we have been unable to affirm ourselves and have failed to gain hoped-for recognition. This is especially applicable to individuals who seek applause instead of affirmation or self-realization.

Selecting clothes because the material is indestructible and colorfast may seem practical, but eliminates the chance to enjoy esthetic elegance. This doesn't mean the false elegance we display when applying for a job or trying to make an impression on people. Elegance is decidedly not the cultivated, exquisite allure that only imitates an idol-role.

Esthetic elegance demands two conditions: each individual garment must be expressly selected for its color and pattern, and must be compatible with the other pieces. You may meet these conditions by dressing like a businessman or a *maître d'hôtel*. That still won't make you elegant. Elegance demands a second ability, almost unattainable, involving verve, elan, chic—joyfully risqué and unique. These attributes stem from a dominant joy and an ability to combine form, color, and pattern to create your own brand of harmony. Only by dressing with happiness may you become esthetically elegant.

If you have to ask yourself how to dress to please, to appear well-groomed, elegant, or fashionable, you are a slave to your role. Your temporary pleasure is merely a vain confirmation of your idol-role. The euphoria of your self-affirmation passes more quickly than changing fashions.

Whether you display indifference or defensive fear of criticism for not being up-to-date in fashion, you will find both states to be cheerless. The conformist finds himself on the seesaw of fashion, motivated not by genuine pleasure but rather by a sense of apprehension. He or she fears appearing old-fashioned, unfashionable, unattractive.

Fear of criticism compels many people in managerial positions to wear crisply white shirts and severely tailored suits, not because they enjoy or feel comfortable in such clothes, but rather because they don't want to appear unkempt. The idol-role sets them apart from joyfully esthetic elegance, just as defensive slovenliness or indifference would.

Most individuals observe the same criteria to dress for many occasions. Esthetic elegance of dress is just as evident in leisure-time clothes. Someone who is sloppy in his workaday office clothes is likely to mend a torn ballroom gown with a safety-pin.

We might categorize levels of dress in four groups:
1. Elegance: happily individual and superior combination of dress
2. Well-groomed: conventional role imitation or dashing dress
3. Indifference: unharmonious but clean clothes
4. Unkempt: unharmonious and unclean clothes.

The Dress Style

Dress distinguishes the office employee from the intellectual, the graphic artist from the electrician, the housewife from the cleaning lady, the beautician from the teacher. The reason for these distinctions lies in the differing demands on—and function of—

such different clothes, as well as their style and structure. The well-dressed actress will dress differently than the welfare worker, the well-groomed architect differently than the carefully attired banker.

Four style structures are found on opposite poles:

Traditional and original
Classic and new-fashioned

The Traditional Dress of the "Blue Type" (+Blue)

Costumes and uniforms are tradition-dictated styles. Uniformity of dress is sought after whenever we want to express a togetherness, a cohesion, a community. Wearing a traditional "uniform," whether a peasant dress, a Salvation Army tunic, a nun's habit, drum and bugle corps attire, or a riding habit, is a way of personifying a "higher idea," an ideal.

This "higher idea" can assume many forms. In the case of a peasant costume, it may signify "I am virginal and whoever leads me astray, I want to be his alone, completely." Ideally packaged, this would symbolize faithfulness, a phenomenon historically tied to the color blue (i.e., true-blue).

If we affect a uniform of bodily freedom, unfettered dress, and natural expression, we are partisans of "bare existence," i.e., nudity. Our higher ideas signify that nature is naked and therefore nudity equals nature in its original state. Whether peasant dress or stately, stodgy banker's attire, traditional clothes manifest the idea of unity, harmony, natural simplicity, of belonging together, continuity, and faithfulness.

Unique Dress of the "Red Type" (+ Red)

The creatively productive "Red Type" is enterprising esthetically, apt to enthuse and inspire, and adventuresome. An esthetically original woman, for example, is one who'd fashion a swimsuit from a piece of chamois leather that was meant to clean windows. An esthetically original male demands made-to-order shirts with a unique collar of his own design.

If you sew according to a standard paper pattern, you may pat yourself on the back (but not too much!). You're an original person if you prefer a unique design; you don't imitate a stock pattern. Whether you implement the design yourself matters little. Originality expresses itself in the selection and combination of attire.

If you have mastered the esthetic level of elegance, you are implicitly original. However, not every original creation is esthetically elegant—for example, a little breadbasket with feather trim used as a hat. That borders on absurdity. The bachelor whose socks have holes in the toes, and who puts on a second pair with holes in both heels, never becomes esthetic, even though he'll be original all his life.

Genuine originality reveals an intellectually psychic attitude that distinguishes itself by enthusiastic pleasure, open-mindedness, and erotically adventuresome intensity.

Classic Attire of the "Green Type" (+Green)

"Classic" is a concept that denotes attire tailored according to strict rules of conservation form and color.

Devoting yourself to classic ideals means observing "rules of dress." Being underdressed would shame that person. Each item of dress that retains habitual style, despite ever-changing fashions and fads is a "classic." In that sense, a man's trousers may be cut as classically as a black tuxedo or an unpretentious cocktail dress.

As a rule, classic colors are subdued rather than variegated; the classic cut is mostly simple. If you want to look classy, you'll have to be conspicuous by your discrete dress. Classy dress is achieved by consistent appearance, perpetuating the impression of prestige we want to create. Classic style denotes a wish to "be someone." Dressed this way, an individual commands attention or even respect. He expect to be accorded the dignity of a special personality, fancying himself on everyone's list for New Year's felicitations and birthday wishes.

Fashionable Dress of the "Yellow Type" (+Yellow)

New fashions bring about changes in color, pattern, design, and cut. Fashion thrives on change. Fashion is a convention in itself, the convention of the new. It opposes conservative convention and propagates a different one: the new fashion. It prospers on the allure of the new, on the urge for change.

Whoever seizes on new fashions is not original as such, but rather fond of change.

But making a fetish out of being different isn't original, either.

We do have to admit, however, that such a person would *like* to be original. A desire for originality isn't unusual, but can become extreme. If the desire to impress becomes overwhelming, it may hide a secret fear of being ignored.

Beside the four *idol*-roles:

tradition and originality
classicism and fashion

stand four *defensive*-roles:
uniformity and change
conservativism and extravagance

The idol- and defensive-role can be expressed in the same direction of style, the same manner of dress. Only the motives differ: a desire for self-affirmation ("Boy! Am I ever fashionable now!" or fear of criticism ("As a businessman, I can't afford to wear what I'd really like").

We differentiate between four directions of style which we employ as defensive roles:

Uniformity of Dress of the "Red Defensive Type" (—Red)

Inspiration and authenticity are prerequisites for originality. The former requires mental effort, the latter maturity. If these efforts are too great, we are content to glide along in conventionality. Our limp heart beats only for conformity and uniformity. Our familiar style of dress seems like a sheet of wrapping paper used year after year for our lunch sandwich. Our necktie, a matter of indifference, is merely loosened at night, slipped over the head and tightened in the morning. One fine day it simply disintegrates, soiled and aged.

Variation in Dress of the "Blue Defensive Type" (+Blue)

An aversion against all repetitiveness (refusing to wear the same dress twice in the same company, or being afraid of meeting someone wearing the same dress) is fear of continuity, based on fear of emptiness, of loss or lack of allure (—blue). It bespeaks unrest, a hesitation to relax and "let yourself go." The urge to change can be measured by the size of your clothes closet and the number of your suitcases.

A person who holds his audience spellbound by a steady change of costume, or changes his appearance like a chameleon, is under the impression that he can appear as an interesting and original personality, merely because of such variations.

The spectator may be astonished by this wealth of transformations, just as he would be fascinated by a kaleidoscope. But hardly anyone would expect to find a *genuine* personality shape behind this colorfully changeable image.

The Conservativeness of Dress of the "Yellow Defensive Type" (—Yellow)

Conservative posture protests against "eroticism" and carefree spending, while fashion constantly changes, sometimes erotically, always boosting economic consumption. That is why businessmen opt for conservative garments—to prove the fickleness of fashion. Behind such conservative propriety is the will to maintain regularity, constancy, order, and security. External order is seen as the way to achieve an inner system.

A conservative manner of dress is chosen by individuals who prefer *their* order over the discomfort of reality. This lets them function in accordance with *their* role and *their* rules of the game. Their faces reflect self-consciousness, anxiety, and a sour keep-smiling attitude; they subjugate themselves to a stern taskmaster in their determined sense of duty.

The Exclusivity of Dress of the "Green Defensive Type" (—Green)

If we raise our demands to a level that others can't keep up with, we become exclusive. Exclusivity is a pecularity, a pecularity of high quality. If we aspire to be peculiar just to be different from others —wearing one's hat backwards, or burping in the face of a piece of art—we aren't different, but extreme. We don't satisfy criteria of quality, of extraordinary achievement.

Exclusivity doesn't require an original idea, or

organization of thought or action. It's an expression of esthetic judgment and choice. Exclusivity is not tied to steep prices, but to the ability to judge esthetic perfection and selection of the unusual.

Contrary to the extreme behavior requiring spectators, exclusivity allows room for subjective pride. There is erotic pleasure in the discovery of beauty—elegant shoes from Milan or a unique cashmere pullover from London. The "Green Defensive Type" turns to esthetic objects, jewelry, clothes, furniture, or *objets d'art* for this satisfaction. He may use this search for esthetic beauty as an alternative to an unsatisfactory relationship at home. To dress exclusively, you must be demanding and choosy, which creates inward tension because of the pressure to realize these ideal demands. This person frequently gets into situations of duress and impairment. He often gets stuck in a mental dead end because he wants it both ways—free choice with no sacrifices. He retreats into exclusivity, his own private "heaven on earth."

The following combinations depict the relationship between the four idol-roles and the four defensive-roles:

Idol-role		Defensive-role	
(+Blue)	traditional	(−Red)	uniform
(+Red)	original	(−Blue)	alternate
(+Green)	classic	(−Yellow)	conservative
(+Yellow)	fashionable	(−Green)	exclusive

These eight role-characteristics appear singly as well as in combination. We frequently find the idol-roles and the defensive-roles combining: fashionably (+Yellow) and extravagantly dressed adolescents who want to demonstrate their independence to their elders (combining separation-urge and rebellion); classic dress (+Green), and conservative dress (−Yellow) melding yearning for security with a kind of wooden dignity.

On the other hand, we may find several idol-roles in tandem. Genuine originality (+Red) can join with new fashion and style (+Yellow) in a playground of ideas. Dressing fashionably and originally can make it easy to meet new people. Still, this new relationship may not grow into a fruitful one.

Apparel can protect the torso or decorate it. The protective cover can also become decorative packaging when it comes to an article of beauty and pleasure with market value. A pack of cigarettes is designed to convey a specific image indicating a level of prestige; it thereby addresses a target audience. Similarly, we humans dress according to a specific image-role to establish a rapport—albeit subconsciously—with a target audience of *our* choosing.

A conservative business executive may distrust the casual dress of his advertising director, who places himself in a different social grouping. Semiconsciously but quickly, we manage to classify a person's social status by dress.

If you're familiar with the psychology of colors and shapes, you'll recognize the different emotional signals a person emits with color nuances, combinations, patterns, and fabric quality. If you're familiar with emotionality, you'll sense how precisely and completely we each recognize and judge these same subconscious signals. This holds true even if the other fellow's reaction is simply "likable" or "disagreeable."

Chapter 4

Sex Symbols and Genuine Love

Most of us are better equipped for business, success, and wealth than for genuine love. That's one reason we regard "love" as a business, an exchange of our own consumer values (beauty, youth, intelligence, possessions, sex, social standing) against the consumer values of our partner.

If you are this calculating, you don't love. You are merely impressed with the role your partner represents. You admire in your partner such advantages—beauty, intelligence, social values, and possessions—as you'd like to have for yourself.

If you desire and are impressed by these things in your partner, you are "in love"—you do not *love*. You *imagine* you've found your great love. But that has no connection with genuine, true *great* love. Even worse, this kind of "being in love" is a hindrance to genuine love.

Whatever you'd like to be or to achieve, whatever is lacking in *you*, you hope to receive from your partner. The hoped-for profit may arrive, but love remains lacking, and disappointment will replace it. You're apt to seek a new partner, still with the same profit-goal in mind. Your disappointment will repeat itself. The lonelier, and therefore more demanding, we become, the more intense will be our hunger for love. We're frequently apt to anesthetize our lack of love in a relationship by sexual excesses. Sexual satisfaction, perhaps by aggressive subjugation of a partner, can easily grow into dependence, jealousy, or passion. Yet it is still not genuine love.

Freud, the renowned psychologist and sex researcher, established a principal theme of psychology which barely touches on love. His pupil, Theodor Reik, then Erich Fromm and others, seemed to prove that genuine love occupies a vital place in psychology. Despite this, some psychiatrists and laymen under Freud's influence still cling to their own mistaken impression that love is insolubly tied to satisfaction of the sex urge. Love of the heart is thus assumed to be a sublimation of an impeded sexual urge, a kind of detour.

Thus, if we don't make love an object of barter in the emotional marketplace, the question will no longer be: "Where can I find true love and a partner who'll love me absolutely and totally?" but rather: "How capable am I of genuine love."

Few individuals can fulfill the conditions of

genuine love. The majority treat their great love as a temporary illusion; they never master the art of love and loving. If we're ignorant of the *ideals of love*, we can never learn the *art of loving*. Love will remain illusory. Psychologists trained in the Freudian school of sexual orientation don't believe in these ideals.

Theologians with a pious embarrassment of sexuality are moralistically opposed to sensuality; they are merely sexually amputated preachers of love. Love without sexuality and tenderness is like a blank piece of paper, a composer's score without music.

If you are dissatisfied, you need and want to be loved, but you aren't ready for "genuine love." Contentment can be learned or acquired. On the one hand, it requires compromise (but not subjugation), on the other, it requires self-confidence and a readiness to give of yourself, to help another. This statement may surprise those who seek an "ideal partner," because genuine love is a result and a consequence of self-realization.

These requisites are difficult to acquire when an appropriate love object won't yield his or her genuine love. The people who are supposed to be our models (a radio commentator or a musical star, for example) are by no means appropriate ones. They can't live up to their public image. Nonetheless, made into stars by publicity, singers, as well as stage and screen actors, are admired as "perfect images" by the public.

Such individuals are often especially immodest, even though they may give a public impression of patronizing modesty. Feeding the tabloids with the most intimate details of their private lives, and even documenting in autobiographies that they are incapable of genuine intimacy (a subject one simply doesn't discuss with strangers), shows their duplicity.

In a society where intimacy is designed to impress others, we may find that true modesty and the ability to love will atrophy. Individuals will be incapable of loving because they use every effort to assert themselves, and even in the most intimate encounter, think only of the impression they create.

As this person is incapable of genuine love, so is the person playing the role of a helpless or self-pitying individual. This role ("I can't live without you!") can be played as a tactic or childish ploy, with appropriate intonation.

Pompous self-assertion and childish helplessness are two roles designed to exert authoritarian influence upon others. Yet, they stifle the development of that person's self-confidence. Confidence in one's strength and readiness to help others are prerequisites to the ability to love.

The feeling of community, of "belonging," of fitting into a segment of society, is emphasized by one's ability to modify excessive demands in consideration of one's partner. That is the kind of relationship we can regard as genuine love. Immodesty, by contrast, is the reason a love relationship may run aground.

Many males believe they're "playing it right" when they appear high-handed and demanding. Misinterpreting the method and meaning of female emancipation, we find numerous females today imitating this counterfeit role of the male. These women are under the impression that emancipation requires an imitation of their male counterpart's immodest behavior, instead of becoming really liberated.

Being modest and unassuming, the prerequisites to contentment and the ability to love is basically the attempt to "fit in" without subjugation or sacrifice.

If we misinterpret the readiness to cooperate, to help, as a sacrifice, we abandon or deny ourselves. Being willing or ready to help or to cooperate out a feeling of love demands no reward. But whoever "sacrifices" himself is secretly calculating; he demands gratitude and some kind of reward.

Every good deed which is performed out of a feeling of sacrifice happens neither in modesty nor out of genuine love. Self-denial is an authoritarian role which tries to force love, gratitude, or dependence ("I do it all for you, so that you love me"). Love cannot be compelled by self-denial. Such coercion derives from immodesty; it stifles love.

Immodesty is most often manifest in the demands which we make of our partner, whether unspoken or implied. We demand excessive and constant attention or recognition. All immodest expectations lead to disappointment, and soon to a resentment of your partner. Symptoms of a subconscious repulsion appear: excessive sensitivity and criticisms, pretense, nagging or resentful silence, reproachful defiance, and spite. An inner barrier against the partner builds, appearing as sexual indifference or resentment. Increasing distance, isolation, and, finally, separation result.

Another ideal, that of inner independence, is

specified in the guidelines for honest loving. Whoever feels dependent on material, sexual, or social demands is apt to cling to a partner because he or she seeks safety and security. If you "love" because of dependence, or if you imagine yourself tied to a partner for the same reason, you're unlikely to find your "great" love. If you feel dependent, you cannot live according to your true convictions, nor can you be open and aboveboard with your partner. If you haven't become inwardly independent, you'll remain fettered, tied, unliberated. You'll exist in your own provisional and short-lived world where all love is extinguished.

I won't go into the numerous false doctrines or mistaken concepts of love of a sexual, material, or social kind, nor those of profit-oriented, frustration-doomed nature. We can nevertheless answer the *secondary* question: "*Who* really would be an appropriate partner to that great love?"

We see that individuals who have mastered the art of independence and contentment, self-confidence and modesty, and who, because of these assets, are tolerant, ready to help, open, and aboveboard, are capable of love.

Great and genuine love is no illusion. But many of us never experience it, and some of us feel it only partially and for a brief time. It is an art which must be learned, exercised, practiced.

The ideals we've discussed here—inward independence and openness, self-confidence and helpfulness, modesty and tolerance—are indispensable prerequisites for a genuine and harmonious love-relationship. They can be "arranged" in a "checklist" by which we monitor our conduct, our attitude, and communion with our partner.

Great love is experienced not merely as sexual partnership, but as genuine communion. It is a complementary part of our whole being and an essential part of our self-realization. With genuine communion, the partners holding differing interests and opinions will tolerate each other. But they'll agree in their mutual ideals. In that—and only in that!—total accord *must* exist. Where total agreement on basic ideals prevails, certainty and an assurance of genuine, great love will follow. Genuine *intimacy* is assured by such an accord.

Sex Signals

Sex signals (for example, a display of sexual jokes) are almost always misleading. A person may use obscenity to overcome his inhibitions, or to create a jovial atmosphere in while to transact serious business (an ebullient, jocular insurance salesman would be a likely example). Someone who intentionally creates a sexually oriented mood most often has nothing to offer. If you find yourself in a sexually explosive situation, you'll make the astonishing discovery that this bomb neither ticks, nor is it apt to explode.

What, then, *are* the signals that reveal true eroticism? Would they be the expression of one's eyes, mouth, hands, the posture of one's body, movement, attire, jewelry, or voice? Or are external body characteristics, i.e., hair color, hair growth, breasts, legs, stature—are they the real hints of erotic and sensual conduct?

First we'll have to eliminate all *misleading* indicators. Our color and shape tests indicate that we all respond with predictable emotions to certain colors and shapes. A square, for example, indicates a kind of tense stability, clear and systematic orderliness, and persistence. A rosette of softly flowing, undulating lines engenders a feeling of relaxation, coziness, and comfort. All shapes and colors we perceive, whether abstract or physical—as abstract circle or a round bosom, black printer's ink or ebony female hair—produce specific and precisely definable sensations. We all understand that these sensations exist only *within* ourselves, and that they occur neither in black ink nor in the circular shape as such.

If certain attractions delight the individual, it then becomes difficult to comprehend why a firm, round bosom or a female's black hair should release sensations only in the beholder, that they do not in themselves signify anything about a person's character.

Nevertheless, an individual's psychic make-up and life-style will be revealed to a great extent by the physique. It may be athletic and muscular, slender, or well-rounded and tending toward obesity. In other respects, expressive movements and facial expressions are of more practical value than body shapes as signals of character.

Young or inexperienced persons may forego sensitive observations, taking their cues instead from purely external physical particulars. A young girl, for example, may be ready to fall in love with any man who is tall, slender, muscular, and dark-haired. Some males become lustful the moment they encounter their "leg-breasts idol" and these sex signals of a primitive nature are enough to cause physical reactions.

We won't delve here into such biologic "key provocations," but we'll examine the emotional postures and related signals by which an experienced person can interpret the erotic and sensual behavior of a sex partner. He won't jump to conclusions merely on the strength of physical (bodily) characteristics such as hair color or thickness of lips. Rather, he'll evaluate the sum total of *all* expressions realistically.

Aside from anatomic and physiologic function, sexuality is a role-conduct and therefore an expression of emotionality. It therefore becomes vital to make emotional relationships intelligible, to understand the "love-shapes," and to be able to link them with their appropriate sex signals.

Despite a plethora of sex literature, vagueness and obscurity prevail pertaining to emotional relations, "love-shapes," their idol-role and defensive role, and combinations of these manifestations. You should therefore refer to page 97 to discover a comparative table of such symptoms.

We distinguish between four shapes of love as structures of emotional relationships:

Sympathy (blue)
Sexual body allure (red)
Commitment (green)
Eroticism (yellow)

A relationship between partners may involve all

four of these forms, or only three, two, or just a single one. A relationship may consist only of sexual attraction, or it may be a matter of mutual sympathy and have neither sex, eroticism, nor an eventual commitment in mind. We use "sympathy" in the sense of understanding and empathy, as expresses in "Christian love." Thus a teenager who is wild about a teacher or a matinee idol may experience erotic enthusiasm without being capable of sympathy and without considering a commitment. That same teenager may even shrink back from the very *idea* of a sexual encounter.

Sympathy

The love-shape of sympathy (blue) corresponds to trustingly sympathetic, understanding empathy. It is always joined to the Greek concept of *agape*, or what we know as Christian neighborly love, leaving sex and eroticism "across the way."

The aim of sympathy is communion, trust, and understanding. Sympathy expresses itself as patient good will, such as a mother would demonstrate toward her child. Sympathy does not demand.

Harmonizing
Idol-Role of the "Blue Type" (+Blue)

Signals of the kind of sympathy allied to harmony are the serene, slightly subdued glance of a partner's eyes. The pupil is constricted. The lips are closed softly. The corners of the mouth are horizontal. The tongue reposes broad and relaxed in the mouth. The head is frequently tilted slightly forward and to the side, as if one were listening to music. The entire body is in a state of relaxation. Movements are generally slow and quiet. Hand motions are not possessive but rather as if one were tenderly touching. Fingertips of both hands are touching or softly surrounding an object, as if one were holding a glass in one's hand while the thumb caressed the glass. The hands may rest on a horizontal surface or be allowed to dangle at one's side. Speech is serene, the voice sounding soft and low, never loud.

Dress may be most conventional, traditional, well-kept; solid colors may be preferred to strong patterns. If any jewelry is worn, it will be very little. It'll be either traditional—a souvenir or an heirloom —or something esthetically selected. Hairdo may be long, but is frequently pinned on top.

Bodily structure (which is always a doubtful signal) may be rather round, plump, and cozy.

Agitating, Defensive-Role of the "Blue Type" (—Blue)

If the "Blue Type" senses emptiness and boredom—forerunners of an impending loss of allure —that frustration will drive them into a state of restlessness. This dissatisfaction will also cause irritability. We now have a condition which psychiatrists recognize as a classic state of "agitated melancholia" (—Blue). To fill the void of missing feelings, we can increase one of three remaining forms of love: bodily or physical allure, illusory eroticism, or the need to dominate in a commitment. Signals of such agitation are quickly darting glances, irritated movements of body and hands (finger drumming, winding a lock of hair around a finger, picking at clothes), or a hungry sucking-smoking of a cigarette. The tongue makes sucking sounds against the teeth, frequently causing bleeding of the gums. Speech alternates from fast to halting, ever stuttering.

Sexual Body Allure

Bodily allure (Red) is sexuality in the narrowest sense. But this "love-shape" is not limited to sexual organs; the skin's sensitivity (with emphasis on the "erogenous zones" such as the nipples) is subject to excitement as well. Increasing titillation causes an intensive involvement of the entire body; it is sensed as excitement. Such a sensation is tantamount to a feeling of happiness. Excitement grows into tension, the tension becomes excessive until it dissolves into orgasm.

Bodily attractiveness or allure is most often released by physical contact. The criterion is, of course, whether or not a nervous thrill or sensation is evident at the point of contact. That's why body contact isn't an absolute requirement; words and images may cause excitement in specific body regions as well, and lead to orgasm. By dint of such imagination or conception, it may be said that a particular body location has been touched "from the inside."

Touching
Idol-Role of the "Red Type" (+Red)

Signals of readiness to touch, to personify the love-shape of physical allure (+Red) are excitement and increasing tension. The sympathetic nature of this excitation causes the pupils to enlarge. In the case of excessive agitation, vision and eye focus become erratic, and the eyes dart about, unfocused. As soon as tension sets in, the nostrils flare out, the lips part ever so slightly, the tip of the tongue moves forward and up—first behind the teeth, but as soon as self-control diminishes, the tongue emerges as it would in a "soul kiss." The tip turns upward and wags from side to side in excitement. The head is held straight, never tilted. Depending on the degree of excitement, the tilt of the head continues to rise and eventually moves backward and to one side. The entire body becomes more rigid. Movements are agitated; the hands appear to grasp and move an object. This is one reason a smoker likes to hold a cigarette in this setting. Speech quickens and gets louder.

The sex signals of bodily allure include clothing. Body contact is replaced by "optic touch." Women may refer to a man's optic contact as "undressing me with his eyes." Clothes are used as visual stimuli. Body shapes are emphasized through attire (high heels to elongate the legs, a tight pullover to accentuate the breasts, tight slacks to emphasize buttocks). Colors are lively, variegated, and contrasting. Patterns are large and lively as well. Typical figurations are leopard spots, free-shape and contrasting ornaments. Hair styles are not too long, mostly free-falling. Jewelry appears obvious, plentiful, and inviting to touch.

Physical stature or bearing in this situation are of no importance. The tendency is toward the muscular.

Moralizing
Defensive-Role of the "Red Type" (—Red)

Self-admiring, superior-feeling, self-pleased people are apt to suppress spontaneous sensations of lust, finding them disturbing. If physical attractions aren't "acted out," but subdued out of a sense of shame or propriety, they become irritants, causing disgust and leading to excessive provocation. Every sensation which can be interpreted as lascivious desire will be devalued by criticism, we "moralize."

The signals of a moralist who represses such desires are plainly evident in his morose and wretched facial expression. The surly, pinched, downward angle of his lips are evident throughout the day; you can tell time by their position—you know when it is twenty minutes after eight! Above the nose we detect vertical wrinkles which denote constant strain.

Nobody willingly subjects himself to another's self-aggrandizing moralistic superiority. Children have a hard time coping with authoritarian and moralizing parents for as long as they have to live at home, depending on parents for their daily needs.

Ever since the expulsion from Paradise, humans

recognized that they were naked, had nothing decent to wear, and were ashamed of it. Moralizing to one-self and others has been a lust-substitute since the dawn of history.

If we add the demands of a bond (+Green), intolerance shows its consequences. It can develop into self-disciplining, self-chastisement, disapproval, or even flogging of others. Wearing the moralistic straightjacket of shame (—Red) separates erotic (+Yellow) from genuine body allure, bringing about esthetic illusion, or sublimination. Wearing the straightjacket of shame (—Red) only to repress evil lust practices a pious subterfuge designed to achieve harmonious peace (+Blue) without hormonal satisfaction.

The Bond

Green is symbolic for the "love-shape" of a bond, a commitment. It is the shape of a relationship finding fulfillment in interdependence—possessing, and being possessed. A firm commitment strengthens the social structure; it is useful legally. The family is a legal "cell." A love relationship is sanctioned by a legal bond. The inmates of a *love* cell call their institution "marriage," and distinguish themselves by their voluntary commitment from inmates of a *prison* cell. The bond replaces uncertainty with a lack of independence. The bond is the exchange of isolation for dependence. Admittedly, the bond—like every contract—must benefit *both* partners. The cost of such mutual usefulness is fixed; a bond (green) and eroticism (yellow) are antagonists. The desire for a bond is realized at the expense of erotically "romantic" love.

Focusing Idol-Role of the "Green Type" (+Green)

Demanding a bond as sole condition for a partner relationship is a desire to dominate your partner. To wield power over one's partner, to exercise mastery by virtue of the marriage bond or through an emotional tie, is a sign of an individual who needs self-assertion. The same person knows inwardly that he or she is unworthy of love. He will criticize, nag, and carp about the appearance (hair or clothing) or behavior of a partner, demonstrating a know-it-all superiority with quick reproaches disguised as care and consideration.

People seek salvation in love. Hence they're frequently misled by a kind of hypocritical love which is in reality only a disrespectful demand for power. They endure schoolmasterly patronizing because "people *mean* well." They excuse humiliation because of their own dependence.

Even jealousy is misinterpreted as a "sign of love" because of the desire for a bond. A jealous person wants to possess their partner, but knows secretly that this won't make him *deserving* of love. Instead, he finds it difficult to believe that the partner could love *him*, and this causes him to distrust his own emotion. He becomes jealous. Jealousy is only an imaginary loss of love. If the love-partner in fact *does* turn away to focus on another, disappointment sets in. Jealousy can also *accompany* disappointment, when the demand for possession coexists with the knowledge of one's own lack of amiability.

The love-shape of a bond is intended to anchor, to tie down the partner. Signals of such an anchoring bond are a patronizing attitude regarding the partner's opinion as inferior. We won't let him finish a sentence, we cut him off, we point out obvious facts during a drive in the car—things he can see and judge by himself.

To recognize the demand for a bond, look for compressed lips, a straight and horizontal upper lip —frequently of small size. The look is clear, straight, and testing, the lower jaw may protrude as in overbite. Pressure on the teeth may cause the jaw muscle to flex from the lower jawbone to the temples. Chewing motions are plainly visible at the rear angle of the lower jar. The tongue will press obliquely against the teeth in an embarrassing situation. The head is held level. Because of a defensive situation, shoulders are slightly elevated. This causes a slight muscular stress in the back of the neck which can lead to a headache. Legs are frequently crossed, sometimes ever entwined in corkscrew fashion. Movements are measured, frequently stiff.

A most obvious signal is the pointing index finger. It either touches the target person horizontally like a fencing foil in lunge, as if to penetrate that person with one's opinion, or the finger points heavenward where we imagine goodness and truth repose, making it clear that we speak in the name of the Absolute, of objectivity, and of eternal truth.

Speech is slow. Words are evenly spaced and clearly accentuated.

Body structure may be slender. Attire can be classic or conservative. Colors are subdued, patterns striped or plaid. Females may sport artful hairdos, even lacquered hair. Jewelry is mostly conservative and shows wealth; weighty gold collars, pearls, sapphires and diamonds. The commitment, the bond, the wish to anchor one's partner, is frequently the final love shape which remains forever in a partner relationship and causes lasting wretchedness.

Emancipating Oneself
Defensive-Role of the "Green Type" (—Green)

The tie inherent in a bond (+Green) impedes self-realization and may be felt as dependence and compulsion or pressure (—Green). We want to be rid of these sensations; we want to emancipate ourselves (—Green). Many individuals find this necessary decision very difficult. Not only must they find a way out of a dead end, but frequently they sense that they are "leaving a gilded cage." Women, for example, consider it insurmountably difficult to reach professional, material, and mental independence once they have submitted (because of children) to a dependency-bond.

Totally and physically emancipation is possible as well. We withdraw from the bond of communion with the partner, we "break out." We are emancipated until, finally, we don't own an accounting to *anybody*. We don't leave any traces.

One form of the drive to emancipate oneself, [(if it happens in erotically idealized "love-form" (+Yellow)] is to act the "unconcerned flirt." This is based on the fourth type of conduct discussed by Freud: the exploration seeking erotic stimulus in the visual. "Optic allure" (body shape, pinup gal, striptease, pornography).

Emancipation (—Green) makes a vigorous and energetic go-getter of the individual aiming for sexual body allure, the lustful touch (+Red). But an individual (—Green) seeking merely to sidestep decisions and to find comfort and satisfaction (+Blue) plays along out of sheer compliance whenever sexual demands crop up. Conversely, men and women conduct themselves in a *sexually* repelling manner whenever bond-repulsion, emancipation (—Green) and moralizing allure-repulsion are combined.

We're all too familiar with emancipation (—Green) and simultaneous "clinging" (—Yellow), which we recognize as hopeless dependence, subjection. When the urge for emancipation (—Green), is experienced with a desperate need for liberation from a boring and unsatisfying emptiness (—Blue), we want to turn completely away from that relationship. We "depart without a return ticket."

Eroticism

Plato tells us that man once had a spherical shape and could jump so high that the gods in the heavens felt disturbed. To end this frolic, spherical humans were cut in two, and one half has been searching for its counterpart ever since. Yearning for love dominates humans; heavenly aspirations are simply absorbed by a more earthly yearning for completeness—the longing for love.

The yearning for completeness, for the ideal which we ascribe to the loved one, is referred to an "crystallization" by Stendhal: "When a twig (*The Salzburg Branch*) is immersed in saline solution for a time, crystals will begin to form on it. The wooden branch is no longer visible, only the glittering crystals which surround it. In our imagination, we attribute admirable traits to our beloved, and we subsequently view that individual like the twig hidden by crystals, an as idealized being."

Freud's pupil, Theodor Reik, described in *Sex and Love* the reasons we idealize a partner:

> Whoever possesses those qualities we'd like to see in ourselves (beauty, intelligence, attractiveness, popularity, self-assurance, being uninhibited), that person becomes the idealized love partner, e.g. the "ideal" love partner. Whatever I consider my own insufficiency and which secretly scares me, irritates me in others as particularly intolerable. Conversely, I admire and idealize those who distinguish themselves through strength and superiority in those areas in which I feel weak and insufficient.

The love-shape of the erotic ideal-formation reached its peak in the medieval culture of the wandering minstrel era, in the ideal of romantic love. Nowadays it approaches its lowest point because sexual liberation discourages not only illusion, but idealism as well. For centuries, natural sex has been suppressed by Christian moralizing and sanctimonious self-delusion. Nature "in chains" emphasizes delusion, illusion, and lies. Suppressed sexuality begins to boil and ferment. This bubbling foam is referred to by Freud as "sublimation." A culture distilled out of repressed sex is a "plastic" one.

For centuries, embarrassment over sexual lust has prevented people from being spontaneous and honest. Embarrassment, pride, and irritation have their origin in that situation. At the same time, sexual illusions—intensified through sexually oriented literature and promotion—form barricades between humans. It isn't a case of human beings meeting naturally face to face, but rather men and women hiding behind prestige signals, seeking a tactically proper approach.

Role signals that are supposed to be attractive—the car meant to impress, profession, title, property, social influence—are all idols opposed to the ideals constituting the core of erotic love. Ideal erotic love is not necessarily Stendhal's illusionary crystallization, but rather the totality of self-realization in a partner relationship, as described by Plato. It is an inspiring "completion" experienced only through an open-minded and understanding partner (one who is on the "same wavelength"). The ideal of completion and accord—as opposed to the illusory crystallization —is found in a sensible, attentive, emotional, and intellectual companionship; it requires unreserved openness and discussion.

A partner relationship in which this ideal accord is constant and sure would be called "erotic love." Unconditional affirmation and an ability to be open with each other is a form of self-realization feasible only with a partner who is capable of a corresponding attitude; it is frequently a "silent understanding." The erotic ideal is found in frankness and agreement. We symbolize eroticism with *yellow* color.

Idealizing
Idol-Role of the "Yellow Type" (+Yellow)

If you "love" and idolize your partner because of his or her beauty, impressive intelligence, success, etc., you are actually enjoying your own vanity and self-affirmation. This kind of egocentric self-mirror has been known since Freud as "narcissism." Stendhal referred to it as a "love form of vanity." If you regard your ideal fulfilled in external appearances, in social values, in the image of your partner, then you're simply missing the erotic self-realization that results from accord with your own emotional and intellectual manner of living.

Neither commitment nor sex can save you from intellectual or psychic isolation without this essential erotic accord.

Signals of ideally fulfilled eroticism are clearly discernible in a look of frankness, and a radiant expression. The eyes seem to gleam. In erotic situations, eye contact remains steady, as distinguished from the "open look" of lively moving pupils caused by sexual stimulation. As in a condition of sympathy, the lips appear softly closed. They part, as a rule, only after sexual excitement takes over completely. The corners of the mouth point slightly upward. The head is tilted ever so gently. Eye movement tends to lead from below in an upward arc. Body movement and gait are elastic. The hands do not grasp; rather, they fully touch each other. They may let a necklace glide through the fingers in a smooth motion.

Speech is lively. Voice level can be melodious and clear, or drifting. As soon as it begins to sound nasal and squeaky, or halting, it becomes a signal of inhibited eroticism (—Yellow) bogged down in unrequited demands or disappointment; it means we can't find our way to erotic self-realization.

Dress is frequently fashionable. It may be conspicuous though it isn't meant to provoke by its extravagance; it may be rather unconventional attire, coordinated according to personal esthetic taste. Correspondingly, jewelry will be unconventional, sometimes playfully fashionable, at other times having an esthetic peculiarity. The uniqueness documents the erotic search for the ideal. Hair will be well-groomed, even though a hairdresser's artistry may not be obvious. The hair will be worn open and loose or only slightly gathered together, especially if it is long.

Body stature or carriage is not a dependable signal here. It may be slender or plump; it is seldom athletically muscular. It can become rounded if an erotic penchant is disappointed and finds solace in a "sweet tooth" to the point where we speak of "worry fat."

The erotic love-shape aiming for the ideal of agreement or accord often remains an intensive search. It requires an opening up, and a need to remain frank and honest and aboveboard; it keeps us young.

Clinging
Defensive-Role of the "Yellow Type" (—Yellow)

Passion, luck, disappointment—all these sensations take place in the *loving* person, but they relate to the *loved* one. That's why the loving individual can easily imagine that the loved one is producing these situations. We experience our own emotions, thinking that they originate with our partner. This illusory shift of sensation from the self to the partner results in a dependence on that same partner. If we direct all our hopes to the person with whom we *have* a relationship, instead of on the relationship itself, that dependence deepens. We don't try to shape a happy relationship, but instead believe that our partner must *make* us happy. We thus make ourselves and our relationship totally dependent on the partner. Fear of disappointment, of loss of the partner's love, takes the upper hand and negates the erotic and open love-relationship. If possessive demands replace erotic ideals and open-mindedness, we experience a simultaneous fear of losing our partner, which creates gnawing worry. Our "horizon" of living and loving constricts; all our attention is directed to the troubled partner-relationship.

This fear results in "clinging," that classic defense against uncertainty and loss—an attempt to negate the feeling of distance. Like a shipwrecked sailor seeking a firm hold on safety, we cling to security. This stage is *between* unobtrusive and obvious signals. Apprehensive over insecurity, embarrassed and "clinging" (—Yellow), a person may suck in the cheeks, perhaps maintaining that position by gently clamping the inward bulge between upper and lower teeth. In a situation of increased tension, the individual may even injure his cheeks by *biting* into that tissue bulge between uppers and lowers.

More visible is the "clinging" signal in a situation of embarrassment, when the upper incisors appear to bite on the lower lip which is drawn over the lower incisors as if resting on an anvil. An even more intense and aggravated picture is presented when the lower jaw protrudes to let the lower teeth bite into the upper lip.

The "cling" (—Yellow) becomes most intense when one partner, in an apparent embrace, literally *throws* himself on the other. The "cling" may have any of six characteristics, depending on the love-shape it assimilates.

The most pronounced emotional attitude (which Freud characterized as the "anal type") occurs when "clinging" (—Yellow) combines with the demand for a bond (+Green). The bond becomes duress. We demonstrate our own superiority and blamelessness by a show of perfection or nagging. Protecting ourselves against outside influence or criticism, we give an intense and extremely detailed review of our own conduct, asserting our systematic orderliness. We want to affirm our ego and intensify our own feeling of steadfastness and security.

Signals of the demand for a bond, a commitment, are supervising and questioning our partner, demanding accountability, or any other behavior that proves a partner's dependence on us (a simplistic control over household money will do, for starters).

A depressive clinging (—Yellow) to the idolized

partner occurs frequently. Through them, we promise ourselves the fulfillment of all our yearning, harmony, and the loving satisfaction of all our needs (+Blue).

The urge and yearning for safety and security becomes evident in the longing for the *ideal* bond. We expect that faithful devotion will offer a calming security; that it will keep us from becoming lonely or lost, that without it nobody would appreciate us, and we'd be worthless.

We may find ourselves clinging (—Yellow) to a partnership which has become empty, meaningless, and unsatisfying. When agitating dissatisfaction (—Blue) sets in, we still cling to our idealized partner, until we recognize the unhappy liaison.

"Subjection" is the name for such "hopeless dependence," in which we've clung to the partnership (—Yellow) because it offered a certain satisfaction. At the same time we want to emancipate ourselves (—Green) from it because such dependence seems unbearable. Egocentric narcissism and hopelessness are reciprocally interchangeable.

"Jealousy" is the name for the clamps of moralizing (—Red) clinging (—Yellow). When the flowers of the urge to communicate begin to wilt and turn to fear of isolation, jealousy appears.

Clinging is always tantamount to tension, frequently excessive because we want to neutralize our fear of losing our communicability; we want to bridge the distance.

Obvious signals of clinging include the embarrassed (yet sexually significant) pat on the rear, playful nipping as a conscious or overt stimulus of a partner's readiness *to be* sexually aroused. An occa-

LOVE FORMS OF FUNCTIONAL PSYCHOLOGY

Designation	Love-Form	+—Function Idol-Role	——Function Defensive-Role
1 Blue	sympathy	harmonizing	agitating (emptiness, dissatisfaction)
2 Green	commitment	staring	emancipating (narrowness, impeding)
3 Red	physical allure	touching	moralizing (reluctance, fending-off allure)
4 Yellow	eroticism	idealizing	clinging (forlorn, disappointment)

UNDERSTANDING THE SELF AND ROLE-CONDUCT INTERDEPENDENT CONCEPTS

+Blue, —Red	anesthetize, "oral" eating, alcohol, praying, narcotics	+Red, —Blue	stimulating "genital" lustful, wanton
+Green, —Yellow	forcing, "anal" urge to a bond	+Yellow, —Green	exploring, "visual" unconcerned flirt
+Blue, +Green	need to be faithful "we both"	—Blue, —Green	turning away from partner, ignoring each other
+Red, +Yellow	ready to fall in love ideal allure	—Red, —Yellow	jealousy
+Blue, +Red	ready for tenderness	—Blue, —Red	despising
+Green, +Yellow	narcissism vain love of self	—Green, —Yellow	hopeless dependence

+Blue, +Yellow	friendly, considerate thoughtful	−Blue, −Yellow	forsaken, abandoned, unhappy bond
+Green, +Red	gathering	−Green, −Red	repelling
+Blue, −Green	yielding, adapting participation	+Green, −Blue	dominate to assert onself, vamp, frigid
+Red, −Yellow	forced increasing allure	+Yellow, −Red	embarrassed, frightened anticipation, esthetic sublimation
+Blue, −Yellow	clinging, urge to be sheltered	+Yellow, −Blue	seeking, raving, ready for fascination
+Green, −Red	intolerant, moralizing	+Red, −Green	energetic go-getter

sional scratch or playful bite, even a sexually brutal beating, is a means of elevating attraction and allure deriving from the urge to "cling" (—Yellow) and touch.

The lineup of "love-forms" should first include a "readiness to be in love" deriving from an urge to communicate. Amour's arrow is not embedded in a piece of beef; the target will always be "telegraphed" as one's ideal. Only *after* the ideal (+Yellow) has been located, is the arrow released. When the arrowhead has found its mark in the selected body, the situation changes to a specific psychical touch (+Red) to effect an unequivocal physical allure. The readiness and willingness to fall in love occur the instant the allure (+Red) ideal (+Yellow) is located.

The perfidious Don Juan finds it difficult to locate his ideal (+Yellow) in his love interest. The "Tristan" (i.e. Wagner's "Tristan and Isolde"), on the other hand, has trouble being faithful to a like-minded, sensuous person, to hold on to her (to "touch"—+Red), returning unstead to his fantasy idol.

Tristan won't *find* the soul in the body; Don Juan won't *discover* the soul in the body. Both types are unfaithful because they can't bring eroticism and sex into one harmonious focus. Both characters are unfaithful in their own particular ways; they find the faithful Romeo and Juliet on a pole opposite themselves.

The bond is set (+Green) despite all disadvantages and discomfort. Its mutual sympathy (+Blue) finds fulfillment in a limitless, trusting understanding which can overcome all of life's vicissitudes. Its tranquility and harmony (+Blue) find Romeo and Juliet in the final bonds (+Green), and, eventually, in their common death.

The unlimited readiness for an "understanding" (+Blue) and the resultant responsible bond (+Green) are the basis for the need of mutual fidelity.

Chapter 5

The Erotic Language of Jewelry

There are many kinds of jewelry, from sunflower seed necklaces to those with flawless diamonds of many carats. There are just as many ways to display jewelry, from an intimate gold chain around the tummy to a fancy embroidered sticker on your windshield.

But there are *few* reasons why you would want to embellish your own body from head to toe, as there are few reasons to decorate your bed linen or your car tires. The need to be noticed may show itself in a woman who wants to sleep on monogrammed sheets and pillowcases, or a man with an entire row of headlights, searchlights, fog lamps, and other fancy automobile gadgets from exotic countries.

The same urge motivates an African to pierce his nose with a bone ornament, an Indian nobleman to embellish the side of his nose with a diamond, or a Westerner to wear an ostentatious signet ring. Jewelry as a signal depends not so much on the quality of the object as it does on the motivation of its owner.

Jewelry hardly serves a functional purpose. Even if there was *some* usefulness to the concept—the monogrammed bed linen prevents mixups in the laundry, the battery of bumper lights illuminates full width of the road, the signet ring stamps our crest on documents or seals envelopes—hardly anyone will believe that these are the real reasons we acquire the objects in the first place.

It is precisely the uselessness and technical purposelessness of these embellishments that makes them an expressive personality signal; they weren't consciously chosen for a functional purpose.

Because we select acquisitions to enhance our appearance with personal sensitivity and taste, the manner and extent of our erotic life is revealed.

Sensitivity and eroticism are parts of our intimate self; they reveal expectations and relationships which we don't want criticized or analyzed.

In our erotic behavior, as in selecting our jewelry, we seek emotional agreement with our partner. Whatever we intimately express as eroticism is reflected in our taste and opinion related to jewelry. That is why jewelry serves as an erotic-signal as well as erotic expression.

We can decorate our environment, our place of work, and our living quarters.

Objects which we use frequently—our wristwatch, handbag, suitcases, or cars—may all assume a decorative function.

A third concept is the adornment of our own person with appropriate attire and jewelry.

A fourth idea is the decorating of the body with paint: hair color, makeup, a suntan, polishing finger and toenails.

Each of these four concepts is expressed differently by different individuals. One person may apply makeup with professional perfection, while their clothes are disordered and their apartment appears a battlefield. In the case of a "good" housewife, the apartment is the pinnacle of perfection, while her attire may be tasteless and her makeup nothing more than a sour expression.

In this chapter, we'll limit ourselves to a discussion of the *third* aspect, the items of decorative jewelry.

We have to distinguish which item is used to decorate specific parts of the body. The same type of gold chain sends out different messages or signals depending on where it's worn—neck, wrist, waist, tummy, or ankle. The same diamond ring expresses a different signal when worn on the ring finger or the pinkie, if it is worn singly or with a "little brother."

Body jewelry emphasizes an entire body region and not merely the very linited spot on which it's worn. Earclips don't accentuate the ear; they frame the face. A choker doesn't emphasize the neck alone; it stresses the entire head. A bracelet doesn't necessarily draw attention to the wrist, but to the entire lower arm. An ankle bracelet "illuminates" the leg. A ring focuses attention to the entire hand. Each finger has a different meaning of expression. The signal changes from one finger to the next.

The ring finger lies passively indifferent between the longer and sovereign middle finger and the little finger that's ready for an adverturesome "side trip." The ring finger represents the sensitive area of one's character. If a wedding band adorns it, it's assumed you are married. It it's decorated with more ornate jewelry, we characterize the wearer as an emotional individual. If the ring is small and conventionally decorated, we assume that the wearer's relationship to his/her spouse is a commonplace one; it is a cliché relationship.

If the ring is big, excessively decorated, and provocatively obvious, we can assume that we're dealing with an excessive and overbearing person, or even an occasionally hysterical one. The same ring, if worn on the middle finger, markedly increases and dramatizes these characteristics. The middle finger represents the area of self-reliance. The index finger, which is often used to aid our gesturing in conversation, is expressive of initiative. The person who decorates the index finger embellishes his or her impulses, will-expressions, and is assumed to be self-aggrandizing, arrogant, and presumptuous (Henry VIII, Richelieu, etc.).

The little finger on the outside is easily separated. It is apt to go on excursions of its own. Such erotic or mental sidetrips may be capricious or original. Those who decorate their pinkie use the expression of the ring to show us how he or she expects to demonstrate personal peculiarities. The person wearing a conventionally set diamond strives after outstanding social effectiveness.

A young woman wearing several esthetically chosen matching, yet unconventional, rings on her little finger leads us to assume that she seeks unique stimulation, that she pursues the esthetically attractive and extraordinary, that she is curious, and "collects" new impressions with sensitive attention.

What kind of signal is a slim gold chain girding the waist? How about the ankle bracelet? Some models claim they wear a hip-hugging chain to detect the slightest change in girth or weight. But flesh isn't all that's put in chains that way. Lecherous looks are supposedly attracted by baring the body in this manner. The gold chain becomes a means of coquettish attractiveness. The golden anklet isn't a secret symbol of lesbianism, as some would assume. It is rather a signal of full-blossomed and sexual body awareness. If you adorn not only your face and hands, but your legs and feet as well, your entire body becomes a sensitive symbol of desire.

If we examine the motives of people who adorn or decorate themselves, we also have to ask why *some* people don't devote any attention to these frills. Adorned with jewelry and embellished with makeup is the way *some* want to appear before their environment, while others want to seem as plain and "natural" as possible.

The former (considering the cultural habits of the female) want to introduce themselves with emotionally appropriate jewelry; they want to be acknowledged as "individuals." The latter, however, the plain and unadorned "naturals," want to be recognized for their personality without material signals.

Craftsmen and business people judge external appearances with an objective and functional attitude. On the opposite extreme of the spectrum, we find richly decorated individualists with their own ideology. The desire-denying monk is emphatically unadorned. The ultra-conservative soul, imagining himself unattractive and in an atmosphere of self-deluding inferiority, avoids even a trace of jewelry.

Forlorn females who imagine they're deserted, lost, or betrayed, or those who lack a partner to satisfy their needs, simply don't feel they have to make themselves look attractive by the external means of jewelry. But they *will* reach for the glitter the very moment a new love (or receptiveness to one) appears on the horizon.

If you're prone to decorate yourself with jewelry, your intimately erotic motives may fall into one of these four categories:

1. aspiring to security
2. aspiring to prestige
3. aspiring to sexual allure
4. aspiring to the ideals of beauty and accord

These four totally different motives engender the choice of four radically different types of jewelry. Since different needs have to be satisfied, the jewelry will be distinguished by material, size, design, workmanship, or artistry. Shape and color increase in importance as motives, needs, and emotional expressions charge. Monetary value is important only when there's a desire to show prestige.

"Small Treasure" Type of Jewelry
Aspiring to Security—the "Blue Type" (+Blue)

It's no coincidence that jewelry is most often small. Anything small and weak, any object that needs the kind of care a baby does, requires love and attention. That same emotion governs those individuals who regard their possession as a love-deserving treasure. They seek and admire the kind of jewelry they believe has been created with love, endless care, and patience. This happens predominantly with antique or traditional jewelry which was produced with much emotional attention to form and technical expertise. We find ourselves admiring its loveliness. Lovely jewelry, however, needn't be at all expensive. In some cases, especially in native crafts, jewelry may be made of ordinary metal, ceramics, semi-precious stones, wood, or fruit seeds or pits. The individual who appreciates the care and love, the attention and patience that have gone into the making of such a piece, recognizes these attributes as symbols of concern and security.

The meaning of a teddy bear to a child (replacing the maternal relationship) is similar to the meaning of precious yet small jewelry to an adult.

Frequently, small precious jewelry is round or rounded, of braided garlands or circles. Typical colors are sapphire blue and ruby red. This type of jewelry is preferably worn in the vicinity of the heart, often as a necklace or pendant, and frequently as a brooch on the chest. The symbolism of a cross (horizontal—tranquility; vertical—stability; right angle—steadfastness) represents security as a religious haven. That may often be the reason why girls whose moral conduct is less-than-Christian, and those who need safety and security wear a highly visible small cross on a necklace.

Prestige Jewelry
Aspiring to Validity of the "Green Type" (+Green)

Expensive jewelry is a smart capital investment with a risk factor diminished by its many uses. Jewelry as capital investment has the advantage of being a present for one's wife, displaying her in opulent finery, and at the same time demonstrating wealth. This kind of orgiastic enjoyment of one's possessions has turned prestige jewelry into a confession of "high snobiety." As obvious as a dog wearing his collar, a "fine" lady wears her pears when she goes out. As necessary as the wooden toothpick in a club sandwich is the glittering tie pin worn by the "lord of the manor."

Wobbly and massive as a double chin, m'lady's heavy gold bracelet catches our eye. Bored as a fish eye, the glowering solitaire stares at us from many a ring finger. They're all displayed in the subliminal hope of encountering an envious glance here and there.

Conventional jewelry, a pearl ring, a diamond, a sapphire in a diamond setting, gold bracelets, and necklaces—they're all signals of a demand for prestige. This desire is satisfied with casual comments, or an occasional allusion to sexual matters. However, an attitude that says: "What's small can't be very valuable" shows its yearning for prestige and recognition by draping the entire body in precious jewelry. Then arrogance, haughtiness, and a show-off desire all vie for the spectator's attention.

Prestige jewelry is an attention-getting signal (+Green). The caterpillar covered with mountains of gold and diamonds can develop into a butterfly literally *begging* for attention—our knowledge of human nature tells us that from the beginning.

Prestige aims to impress. It strives forcibly to inform our fellow humans: I *am* what you are *not*, or I *have* what you have *not*. That doesn't require a king's castle, but rather a small sign or signal which informs everyone why we expect them to genuflect respectfully on meeting us.

Little signs are as plentiful as sand in the ocean. Whether Rotary Club or Legion of Honor, baseball insignia or some other sports emblem, everyone who decorates himself with such a prestige signal is saying that he's someone special. And they all have one thing in common: each one is "the" most important individual.

Formative Jewelry
Aspiring to Accord of the "Yellow Type" (+Yellow)

Things we agree with, that live in accord and harmony, we register as "nice." That's why we refer to "nice weather," or a "nice speech." Esthetic beauty, however, doesn't require agreeable taste or personal accord with an object or situation, but rather that the objects harmonize with each other.

We consider a picture esthetically nice as long as its forms, colors, and ideologic content are in harmony with each other. We may even consider a rusty bicycle wheel as esthetically nice, even though a technically functional or esthetically *subjective* point of view may consider it unsightly. Prestige jewelry or alluring jewelry, by its provocative extravagance, is frequently the opposite of esthetic accord.

Jewelry which has been selected because of its esthetic appearance, because of its being part of a harmonious entity, may be referred to as "formative jewelry." It may be earclips selected to match hair style or dress, or it may be a belt with a certain buckle, if colors of slacks and shirt or dress require such a "horizontal connector."

A wristwatch worn like shoes, for utility, may be chosen strictly as a technical chronometer, or it may be an ornament, an adornment of the arm. Whoever wears a diamond-studded watch, a solitaire, or a pearl choker while sailing or on horseback, may have a nautical or equine feeling, but certainly not taste for jewelry.

Whoever uses jewelry to accentuate his or her esthetic appearance pays attention to beauty and to the ideal of harmony.

Esthetic beauty is a personality signal of the individual who is sensitive to the attraction of the environment; the person who cares for the feelings and reactions of fellow creatures in the sense of harmony.

Chapter 6

Idiomatic Language as Expression of Emotional Attitude

You can actually say a lot without saying anything. True? To make a long story short, you need an information specialist to boil it all down to its core. Everything that informs, he calls a "bit" (as in computer language). If you subtract the bits and informative core from a lengthy story, what's left is mere noise or redundancy. Repetitive filler words with no informative value, such as "isn't it?" or "so to speak" or "you know" are signals mirroring the emotional attitude of the individual. You may repeat certain expressions so often in so few sentences that you quickly reveal your emotional attitude and thinking process. Certain expressions reveal far more of your living experience than specific words themselves.

You can say you liked a specific movie with a simple "yes" or with a more verbose "Fantastically nice!", with a plain "no" instead of the more emotional "what a piece of garbage!"

Affirmation or denial may be expressed on different levels of emphasis. The objective "yes" may turn into a more forceful "certainly!" or "precisely!" or "right you are!" A third level changes an affirmation to a laudatory qualification that humors your partner; "first class!" or "A-One!" or "excellent!" You'll cross a substantial threshold going from third to fourth level, from "very good" to "excellent."

The next level expresses your own emotion. "Magnificent," "indescribable," "powerful," "fantastic." The highest level of affectation in answering a question is to inform the other person that you're totally overwhelmed and capable of the most intense emotion; you find something "insanely beautiful," "mad," "crazy, man!", "uncanny." (These affirmative responses correspond to the functions labeled +.)

Even the negative, a denial (the —function) may be expressed in five levels of intensity. The objective word "no" can be intensified for critical judgment as "wrong!" or "impossible!" At the third level, it becomes a disqualification with "bad" or "absurd" or "awkward" or "dumb." As in affirmative reaction, the step from third to fourth level is a major one in negative reactions; it becomes a subjective emotion. Instead of a disqualifying but simple "that's bad" or "absurd," we now have an emotion of indignation: "total nonsense!" or "absolutely beyond discussion"

114

or "terrible" "horrible" "dreadful" "shocking" "hideous," or "a bad scene!"

If we show indignation in a more refined manner, we emphasize our mood with the qualifier "very" as in "very unpleasant." The fifth and highest level of emotion in a denial is total aversion. We are likely to express our displeasure with "baloney!" or the far more forceful "shit!" The frequent use of such epithets, the monotony of unbridled or filthy language, doesn't alter the emotional attitude, it merely signals that the less-than-pleasant feeling has become a habit.

Repetition of meaningless expressions are sure and quick indicators of an individual's emotional level. We can read an attitudinal degree as easily as we read a thermometer, on a scale of $+5$ to -5, from "fantastic" down to "baloney." But emotional posture may be different in different environments. A businessman may spur his employees to greater enthusiasm with criticism; he may "lubricate" the enthusiasm with praise, and his bag of expressions may range from "very disagreeable" to "very good." However, at home when he holds the evening newspaper in front of his face as if it were an open drawbridge, a mere grunt may be the highest accolade he can muster. Describing his girlfriend, his emotional thermometer hits the top. Everything'll be "wonderful" or "incredibly good." But if he's disappointed at this point, it's "terrible" "shocking" or "gruesome." If you have an opportunity to observe someone who, in the same context, affirms a situation quite emotionally and then turns around and denies it just as intensely, you'll find that both expressions (+ and − functions) are on the same level of intensity.

Someone who affirms with "yes, indeed!" will be as emotional or intense when rejecting or denying a situation, by saying "out of the question!" Similarly, praise expressed with "excellent!" on the third level of emotion, we equate with a disqualifier using the expressions "dumb," "unreasonable," "absurd." If you express your delight with "it's a dream!" or "indescribably beautiful!" you'll also negate a situation on the same—the fourth—level of emotion. You'll express disappointment with "frightful," "gruesome," "shocking," "hideous," "atrocious." You'll also label as "totally impossible!" whatever goes against your grain.

If your feeling and emotions raise your expression to the fifth level, and you therefore use such terms as "insanely great!" or "fantastically beautiful!", you'll also express aversion when something disappoints you with "I could puke!" or "damned garbage" or "shit!"

Here you'll find the five emotional levels of affirmation and negation with examples of corresponding idioms. Between these two opposite lies indecision. It may be unemotional and objective ("perhaps" "depends"). However, the seeming indecision ("I don't know, but...") is an expression of an emotional attitude that is a rather revealing signal. If you say "I don't know, but I feel..." then you *are* sure of your opinion but you fear that others won't agree with you, and that they won't share or confirm your opinion.

PHRASES EXPRESSING EMOTIONAL ATTITUDES

Level	Affirmative	Negative
1	*Unemotional:* Yes	*Unemotional:* No
2	*Confirmation* Yes, indeed! Exactly! Right you are! In order! Agreed! O.K. All clear!	*Criticism* Under no circumstances! Not right! Wrong! Impossible! Out of the question! Never!
3	*Praise* Very good! Swell! First class! Excellent! Great!	*Disqualifiers* Bad! Miserable! Inferior! Unreasonable! Dumb! Dilettantic!
4	*Emotional* Beautiful! Wonderful! A dream! Excellent! A fairy tale! Fantastic!	*Indignant* Asinine! Very disagreeable! Completely impossible! Totally out of the question! Gruesome! Horrible!

Indescribable!   Damned!
Powerful!
Heavenly!

5   *Overwhelming*   *Aversion*
    Uncanny!   Garbage!
    Crazy!   Shit!
    Insane!   Kiss my—!

Man was endowed with two ears so that he could distinguish between true information and empty blabber. Behind affected terms like "insanely terrific," "total nonsense," you find self-admiration. Only self-affirmation lassoes the listener, whom we then use as a yes-man with such suggestive ploys as "isn't that so ... Do you understand ... Do you get it?"—all nothing more than shameless demands.

While the Idol-I reflects itself in affectations ("I find that insanely, frantically mad!") the idol-role fishes with such sham questions as "understand? ... isn't that right?" for the listener's confirmation.

Even in playing a denying and defensive role, you're seeking affirmation. But because you can't expect enthusiastic support in such a situation, you resort to objective necessity. Instead of saying "I don't want to," you say "It just won't work." In an antlike society, where the boss has the same conveyor belt mentality as the worker, nobody says "I don't want to because it's not worth it to me," but rather "I have no time." If you really want to, you can find the time, because the top executive has the same 24 hours per day available that the coistered monk has. Time

118

(objective measurement) is a lame excuse for the subjective unwillingness.

TIME AS EXCUSE	
Self-reliance (emotionless) "Yes" "No"	Relation to the environment "It's functional" "It isn't functional"
Idol-I+ Self-affirmation Insanely fantastic Uncannily good	Idol-Role+ Meaning to be confirmed D'you understand? Isn't it true? What d'you know? Get it?
Fright-I Averting one's own helplessness	Defensive role— Denial to be confirmed It won't work. I don't have time for it.

People who hide in anonymous darkness are exposed as if with a photoflash the moment they bare their secret emotions and their philosophy of life through certain idiomatic expressions.

The utterances "whatever will be, will be... You can't do a thing about it" are easily recognized as the resigned attitude of a weak and spineless creature.

But what about the emotional *filler expressions* some of us frequently use—"sure," "naturally," "actually," "somehow?" If we think through such word signals, we become acutely aware of them and they'll greet us in many a conversation as *personality fingerprints.* Instead of analyzing them in their complex structure, we'll arrange them in two rather coarse major groupings. One will be expressions of self-assertion and self-affirmation. The other will be signals of insecurity and self-apology.

Behind the frequent use of "Naturally," "Obviously," ("Of course I thought of that," "Naturally I whacked him a hard one") we find defensive self-assertiveness, i.e., it isn't self-evident that I thought of it, and it isn't a necessity of nature that I gave him a whack. "Naturally" and "of course" are thus used if we expect criticism and we want to avert it in advance.

If you utter such declarations as "Basically," you want to be seen as the high judge pronouncing a comprehensive, all-inclusive verdict. In that case, self-assertiveness becomes conceit and arrogance.

"Basically speaking," "actually," "insofar as" betray a more modest, objectively oriented judgment posture. If a student expresses joy at meeting a member of the opposite sex on campus and says "Actually, I have a lecture from three to four," it's understood that it would be objectively proper to attend class, but if the friend can "... make time to be with me, I prefer to skip the lecture."

Words like "actually" ("Actually, something should be done about it") which are inserted in speech by thoughtful and critical individuals, really mean to say "To sum up, I find it all preferable to the alternatives." If we juxtapose the "objectively proper" with alternate possibilities, we aim for ideal goals and ethical demands.

"Quite simply" is an expression preferred by people who have to convince themselves of their ability to assert themselves and gain acceptance. "Then I'll simply ask him what to do" shows that the speaker is humored by his self-confidence and feels assured that he can pilot his ship through life.

"Honest," "genuine," "truthful," "serious" are favorite expressions of many contemporaries who've discovered their senseless and humdrum existence, qualified it as self-deluding, and, because of this sham, now question their own credibility.

Food tastes "honest and good," wine is "genuinely delicious," and the cheese is a "serious companion" to the wine. They are "honestly enthused." Their signal idioms confirm it: "My statement is equal to my conviction." Their way of living, however, contradicts their conviction. And that's "honestly" regrettable!

There are numerous signal expressions that denote insecurity about things in general, as well as insecurity of the self. "About," "by chance," "so to speak," "to a certain extent," "such as." If we make frequent use of these expressions in our speech, we betray an uncertainty of our subject, and that we don't care to be held responsible for what we say.

"That will eventually be technically resolved . . . That's—so to speak—safe." We had better avoid such hot-air artists.

"Surely," is a band-aid for uncertainty. "Surely we'll have nice weather tomorrow," "surely it isn't quite so bad." In trying to calm our own or others' doubts and apprehensions, we automatically betray our insecurity by the use of such signal words as "surely."

"Practical" or "practically" are favorites of people who feel insecure with theoretically intellectual concepts. They describe the capacity and function of a machine with such inspired brevity as "Then I practically do nothing except turn this knob." The more frequently and unnecessarily we use "practically," the more we really say "I don't comprehend these details; I lack the insight." Because of such shortcomings, we act impulsively.

"Okay," "now then" is the kind of resignation of a person who believes he knows what to do but doesn't believe it's feasible.

"That's the way it is" means that we regret but accept a given situation.

Seeming insecurity or a tactical excuse can also become an expression of self-admiration and haughtiness. The self-styled big shot finally emerges from his office, grabs the hand and elbow of his visitor, and bursts forth, "You'll have to excuse me a hundred times; I had to handle an overseas call first." Even if he'd admit he wanted to be alone to pick his nose, his demand for a simultaneous plea, "You'll *have* to excuse me for being late" becomes a demeaning sham by a person who admires his own importance.

If we keep on begging others' indulgence, if we give the impression that we're indispensable, we think we must be very important. We continue to use this ploy, not to be excused but to be admired.

"I should think..." This is how many of our contemporary mental paupers express themselves. It isn't easy to find among them a person with a firm opinion who'll admit that he may be right or wrong. "I should think that two times two makes four." The emotional posture of the expression "I should think" reveals first a self-denial, and second, an excess valuation of one's own opinion.

"I should think..." really says "my humble disposition won't let me assert anything *subjective*, but *objectively* I can see it the way I now describe it." In other words, we're saying "I'm not expressing a personal opinion but I *am* judging in the name of objectivity." When we hear these words, we know the speaker has left the back door open to retreat if the judgment proves wrong, without having to jeopardize his credibility.

The combination of apparent tolerance and an arrogant presumption of objectivity, the possibility of opportunistic escape, lead us to suspect a vain, cautious, and emotional posture.

"Speaking as president," "Speaking as an officer." The *speaking-as* person pretends to be so modest as to prefer the role of shadow rather than the VIP role their title proclaims. Since most of these pretenders reached their summit salivating for stature, they profess unabashed modesty, and yet place the crown on their heads in a Napoleonic gesture by the use of "speaking as..."

"Excellent, but . . ." is the name of the game. The Romans played it with *divide et impera.* By using the approbation "excellent," we elevate ourselves to the plateau of the benevolent master. Flattered by the laudatory phrase, we are apt to believe the "but" to be a matter of encouraging critique. We hardly anticipate the opposition and denial that follows; the knife in the ribs comes as a disastrous surprise.

"I'd say that's some fresh guy!" We don't mean that he's fresh under some circumstances, but rather incontrovertibly so. The "I'd say" preface is an enigma; it opens the statement to question and doubt. With that kind of opening, we mean that the individual's sass and brashness and nerve are unusually great, that we didn't expect this attitude, that we're surprised.

It would be easier to understand with a slight modification, such as "This is some kind of fresh guy —or do you disagree?" The "I'd say" part is a contradiction, a means to get the listener to agree with us. We use this modifier instead of the shorter statement, "That's a fresh guy!"

"A charming little dress," declares the salesgirl. "How lovely of you to think of my birthday," assures the businessman. "Charming," "lovely" are adjectives that don't qualify the object or the situation; they're undeniably meant to portray one's own involvement and emotion. If you use such words as "charming," "lovely" you declare an understanding *and* you emphasize and demonstrate that your feelings and emotions are involved. If you're liberal in your acclaim, "this is charming . . . That is lovely," you reveal a desire to be liked in return. And if you find yourself using the same words in a mocking or sneering tone, you betray complacency.

The *melody* of speech is difficult to describe without an acoustic demonstration, because the role of a speaker can be determined from the raising, lowering, and stretching of word-end syllables.

You pretend to be wealthy from fear of being thought frugal. By playing the generous individual, you become a spendthrift. The unreasonable demand (+) (the idol-role) and the unreasonable fear (−) (the defensive-role) are all on our debit side as "small vices." The unreasonable demand or expectation ("I want to appear wealthy, totally and unconditionally") and the fearful desire never to seem poor belong together like the outside and inside of a glove. If you want to take off your glove because it bothers you, it's impossible to remove only the inside. Inside and outside, the feeling of fear and the unreasonable demand must be simultaneously discarded.

A "little vice" is something we commit out of apprehension, like lying or taking a sedative; what we omit out of fear is like the inability to make a request or to say no. Such commission or omission is often inimical to our health (such as alcoholism or drug addiction) and sometimes becomes social irresponsibility (like lying or aggressiveness). These acts are judges in relation to self-realization. The accord between conditions of self-realization and moral responsibility, between psychic, basic structures (+Blue, +Green, +Red, +Yellow) correspond in their social application to ethical ground rules.

The ethical ground rules or basic norms (honesty, openness, social responsibility, and respect for private integrity) are social applications of each person's basic psychic structures.

"Whatever promotes optimum living in good, whatever impairs it, is bad." This ethical norm is valid both for the psychology of self-realization and for social responsiveness.

If we assume an idol-role (+) and a defensive-role (−) instead of factual self-realization, we place our basic psychic structure in a counterproductive relationship.

We may not violate any ethical standards in social conduct, but dislike or irritation with others reveals evidence of some small vice in the area of emotion. Even in that emotional aspect we can establish ethical standards, such as "You musn't turn away, or turn a deaf ear," or "Don't pretend to be interested," or "You shouldn't try to make friends with a false charm."

Just as with big, small, and smallest vices, we can detect fear with almost rhetorical questions like "Isn't that so?" "D'ye understand?" "Is it so?", all of which ask whether we're being taken seriously.

Fear, defensiveness, or disgust are basic to every vice. "Disgusting" is the sensation every chain smoker expressed when he took his very first puff. "Disgusting" was the judgment of an alcoholic on first tasting the liquid. Beer has a repugnant taste to the novice drinker. Whisky burns the throat until one is used to it. The drug addict felt insecure on his first try because his mind reacted negatively to the strange sensation. The opium smoker feels truly ill after his initial try. Many enticing activities which eventually become addictive began with a disgust and an unwillingness only gradually overcome. What later on became lust, desire, and addiction brought only fear and resistance at first.

The first time we mount a horse we're apt to be apprehensive, if not downright afraid. Frequently, even the ardent horseman can't entirely conquer his apprehension. The mountaineer or the parachutist masters his inner fear by an overt display of bravado.

When we overcome initial revulsion and fear, and conquer it anew each time, we create a feeling of strength and superiority. As powerful as the fear we overcome—that's how massive our new self-affimation will be.

Individuals who suffer from fear or who are subconsciously motivated by fear desperately need this compensatory sensation of self-affirmation.

Fear and self-affirmation or self-assertion are the poles between which the vices shuttle back and forth. This pendulum is known as passion.

With passion, we can accomplish everything that offers compensating self-affirmation, from a harmless bridge game or crossword puzzle to a foolhardy auto race, from an innocuous urge to clean house to sexual rage. This statement may seem puzzling, since vices like chain smoking and alcoholism don't disclose which kind of fear and self-affirmation they express. But it does not appear that the conquering of fear and revulsion which began as self-assertion is now being continued and repeated as a series of symbolic acts.

In performing every rite—praying, celebrating

Christmas, or even shaking hands—the emotional sense remains constant and the act may be repeated at will.

By repetition we may intensify the motion and turn it into a conditioned reflex. A comfortable and cozy feeling may overcome a marijuana smoker when he merely smells the telltale odor from afar. We make heroes of ourselves by such ritual symbolisms: "Yesterday we really tied one on!" Or perhaps we fancy ourselves experts: "If you don't carry that label, I'd rather do without a drink!" (In fact, both labels come from the same vat!) "If I can't get my brand of cigarette, I'd rather not smoke at all!" (Only two percent of loyal-brand smokers can pass a blindfold test!)

With this extra pretense—boasting of getting drunk or accepting only one particular label—a person shows off so grossly that, by comparison, the average consumer appears a weakling, uncultured, or a boor. Contempt of others is another form of self-affirmation.

The "little vices" are signals of secret fear or apprehension. The kind of vice it is tells the expert which fear it compensates for. The pipe smoker presumably wants to rid himself of a different fear than the cigar puffer or the cigarette addict.

The cigarette smoker is the only one who sucks up smoke to fill the smoke-void (that's the —Blue signal). He inhales warm, tingling smoke into his lungs. Our survey of 6,000 smokers revealed that those who preferred unfiltered cigarettes and dark, natural tobacco, reject dark blue in the color test (i.e. the Lüscher Color Test). Rejection of blue signifies fear of vacuum and boredom. Inhaling obviously shows that the smoker is filling the void with the warm attractiveness of smoke.

The pipe smoker, however, who makes a production out of lighting up before he makes some kind of statement, seeks some firm hold or support for his self-reliance. His apparent insecurity is rooted in fear of distance and void, of being forlorn (—Yellow). He fears loss of influence or importance in his environment. He is especially fearful of social setback or disgrace. Cupping his pipe bowl in his hand signifies his need for some kind of solid security, a strong belief (in God, money, or companions) in order to find harmonious quiet and peace.

The urge to find shelter, the tendency to search for peace and security which leads a child to mother's breast, leads a man to grasp his pipe bowl.

The smoker of long and slender, pretentious cigars is, however, no shelter-seeker at all. He'll "work" his cigar between tight lips. He'll cogitate feverishly without saying a word. He clamps the cigar tightly in his mouth as if to seal off his thinking process from the rest of the world. He'll observe each detail out of the corner of his eye. As a critical and shrewd individual, this Sherlock Holmes won't be cornered. He wants to prove himself and others that he can find his way out of every dead end.

As a defensive gesture, he will reach for his glowing lollipop with a Buddhalike smugness supposedly sheltering him from all irritations. The signal of the fat cigar demonstrates a demand for self-satisfaction. Color tests done on 200 alcoholics (*Busch*) and on clinically treated obese individuals revealed that both groups refused yellow, showing an urge for something concrete and stable (—Yellow) bringing quiet satisfaction and fulfilment (+Blue). "They'll soak it up until they're blue" ... (+Blue). Filling up on food, especially sweets, is a way to anesthetize feelings of an emotional void; we stuff ourselves until we're psychologically sated. Because emptiness or disappointing loss produce unbearable sorrow, such persons accumulate "sorrow fat" by overeating. Overweight is a signal of an attempt to anesthetize dissatisfaction by absorbing solid or liquid replacement.

A husband may work endlessly at his typewriter or hold incessant phone conversations; he asserts himself seven days a week in his work routine. At home, his wife wields her dustcloth like a victory banner, showing that she, too, intends to win the battle for self-assertion. But the secret fear which motivates incessant office work in one person and unending housecleaning in another has its roots in one and the same symptoms.

Sexual excess or fury stems from a different reasoning process. This ritual of self-assertion derives, like most other passions, from fear. In this case it's the fear of estrangement, the loss or absence of an emotional relationship (—Blue). Such encounters result in an agitated and unsatisfying search, not in an emotional relationship. Their purpose is self-affirmation, and that is fulfilled the moment one has "conquered" or exhausted a partner.

Repeated change of partners and sexual liaisons without emotional involvement are frequently an indication of a disturbed emotional relationship with the mother in childhood, or an unsatisfied sibling rivalry believed to have alienated one or both parents.

The individual who turns his stereo to top volume day after day anesthetizes himself with music, just as another does with whisky. Both methods ignore feelings of fear. Such excess is a small vice, and serves as an escape from apprehension. You would have to be deaf and blind not to recognize the incessant assault of rock music as some sort of anesthesia. On the other hand, you would have to be a castrated angel to find musical satisfaction exclusively in Gregorian chant and choral music. Style of music—whether rock 'n' roll, blues, Wagner, Bach, Mozart—is not a factor defining acoustic vices, but exclusivity and excess are. The person who "consumes" exclusively and excessively a specific style of music suppresses fear. This fear is expressed by the character and the stylistic direction of the music.

The four basic fears—fear of unattractiveness, fear of excessive attraction, fear of being hemmed in, and fear of emptiness, void, and isolation—represent differing emotions. They're apt to be expressed in differing musical *styles*. Each style represents a different level of musical *expression*.

As opposed to simplistic popular tunes, we find Bach's "Art of the Fugue." Despite the differing moods and passions of these pieces, they're emotionally related.

Each musical style produces a specific mood and emotion. Music is used as a tool to set both pace and emotion in a department store, an office, at a dance, or a "petting session." The critertia of sexual signals can also be related to musical styles.

Fear of a vacuum, a void, emptiness, deprivation

and boredom (—Blue) can be expressed as agitation and finds expression in rock 'n' roll music. Similar manifestations can be linked to Liszt's *Hungarian Rhapsody No. 2* and many other compositions whose tempos range from *vivace* to *presto*.

Fear of excessive stimulation (—Red), defended against by moralizing, can be satisfied or alleviated by specific styles of music. A church choir, for example, produces modulated and variegated music without rhythmic emphasis. Folk and country tunes share this peaceful and soothing characteristic. Classical pieces with slower tempos fit this group.

Fear of narrowness, of being hemmed in (—Green), of dependence, the yearning for emancipation—all these sensations find their expression in protest songs. Musical styles which are rhythmically accented (e.g. *Carmina Burana* by Orff) but which may be irregular or unhampered in tempo (such as electronically produced background accompaniment) satisfy the need for emancipation.

Stylistic innovations are often rejected as extravagant noise. Classicists rejected any departure from tradition as a sacrilegious offense against the classical composers' art. Thus music expressing a timid attempt at liberated lust is referred to as "scherzo."

A fear of wide expanses, being forlorn or isolated (—Yellow), such as farmers or soldiers might experience, is successfully negated or neutralized by music with a dominant rhythm and perhaps an even monotone and meaningless, repetitious melody. On a higher plane, we find the *mathematically clear and precise* baroque music of Vivaldi, Bach, Handel, and the *concerti grossi* of Corelli have soothing stability.

Superstition is another one of our "small vices." It lies somewhere in a devilish environment between fear of the unknown and confirmation of *supposed* knowledge. Superstition remains a small vice when limited to a belief that Friday the thirteenth is unlucky, and finding a four-leaf clover is fortuitous.

The way we answer the telephone reveals what we expect from the caller and the kind of personality we want to demonstrate to him. This role would be even more explicit and pronounced if our facial expression and gestures during a phone conversation could be observed. Some individuals light a quick cigarette out of embarrassment or inhibition even before they answer the ring.

To gain a measure of insight into the expression, manner, and meaning of dialog, we must recognize certain distinguishing characteristics. By juxtaposing or pairing them, we can arrive at twenty-eight variations of conversation.

The eight criteria are:

tender (+Blue)	hard (−Blue)
low (−Red)	loud (+Red)
articulate (+Green)	indistinct (−Green)
slow (−Yellow)	fast (+Yellow)

The "Blue Type" speaks tenderly and low, frequently relaxed. The "Red Type" speaks loudly and harshly, and is frequently piercing. The "Green Type" articulates and speaks slowly, often haltingly. The "Yellow Type" speaks quickly, and sometimes indistinctly, and sounds muddled.

Loud and well-articulated sounds energetic.
Loud and quick appears booming.

Loud and soft impresses as sonorous.
Soft and quick appears winged and soaring.

Soft and articulated sounds concerned and deliberate.

The rest of the speech structures can be interpreted with equal facility. The search for safety is characterized by a soft (+Blue)—and supressed, slow (—Yellow)-sounding pattern; it sounds childish and twangy, nasal. The individual who behaves defensively out of fear of failure speak softly (—Red) and inarticulately (—Green); they mumble.

Chapter 7

Characteristics of "Small Vices"

"You mustn't" is the cold water that's frequently poured over bubbling desire. Commands like "you must always show a friendly smile," and pronouncements like "thou shalt not commit adultery" are stakes with which the moralist marks his claim to "Super-I." Behind these lust-barricades he seeks safety and undisputed comfort. But moral points of view are questionable if they advocate only renunciation and not desire. Such moralistic one-sidedness tends to make reason the enemy of desire. "I'd like to, but I don't dare."

But reason and desire aren't mutually contradictory if we follow both paths to their ends, by consciously directing our reason toward those sensations that may cause a contradiction, and, conversely, to those relationships which reason would approve and which would let our feelings unfold to their fullest. If we use our logic and reason to determine the cause of any contradictory feelings, we won't abandon our impulses to deceptive illusions. However, if we are courageous enough to feel our way into a puzzling or contradictory situation, we develop such rational and clear feelings that we'll have no room for illusion. When rationale and feeling assert themselves without contradiction—when both sensations are in agreement—then we possess the assurance that lets us make our own decisions and act accordingly. This condition of maturity is foreign to a neurotic individual, who is unable to reach a decision. The mature person, on the other hand, acts realistically to change a job, a profession, to marry, or to divorce. His acts are based on realism and reality. Because feeling and reason, personal needs, and ethical responsibility are completely attuned to each other, that person exists in inner harmony, deems himself happy, and is adequately successful.

If, on the other hand, a stupid and insensible feeling creates illogical demands, a contradictory sensation takes over and creates apprehension or fear. The consequences can be of momentous importance. The contradiction between reason and feeling is a conflict within and against itself. It makes ethical responsibility to itself impossible and diminished ethical responsibility to others. Such a situation negates openness, honesty, and social solidarity with one's fellow man.

The "characteristics of small vices" don't involve

moralizing; they try to expose fear and unreasonable demands as roadblocks to self-realization or ethical responsibility. It still remains a relatively *small* vice when used to interpret or regulate private, human, and business relationships by astrologic predictions. "It won't make sense because Mars and Saturn are in conjunction . . . He must be the ideal partner; he's Leo, with Libra in ascendance." Even theological superstition existing side-by-side with true religious ethics remains a harmless and *small* vice.

A significant and always *tragic* vice would be an ideology based on emotional insecurity and unconscious fear which isn't satisfied by any personal self-affirmation, but expresses itself in aggression and the use of force.

Instead of mentally pigeonholing "ideologically canned ideas," we need to rid ourselves of prejudice so that we can recognize the ideals to orient and educate ourselves by, to find our own paths to self-realization and mental liberation.

Ideals are fixed human values. They are—like the four directions of the compass—targetpoints that substantiate the path (the method) to deal with any given situation. Each new situation requires new direction, new methods.

Ideologies require for their appraisal an absolute value by which to measure them. Ideologies are intolerant and totalitarian. They aim to convert or destroy all opposing convictions. In the case of ideologic superstition, a catastrophic vice, uncomprehending intolerance is the alarm signal.

Chapter 8

Hobby as Compulsion in Leisure Time

Leisure time is a daily vacation to the wonderland of good fortune. Free of all obligations, we can surrender to the adventure of exploring an immeasurably rich world. Frequently, however, people of a slavish nature will end their day's work by surrendering to the obsession or compulsion of a hobby. One sits laboriously counting the perforations of his postage stamp collection, while another gauges his intelligence on a crossword puzzle: "Horizontal—Verdi opera in four letters; Vertical—composer of *Aida*." One caresses his beloved automobile with a polishing cloth, while another abandons kith and kin to plunge to his midriff in an icy brook, awaiting a fish that's tired of living. Yet a third uses the freedom of his or her leisure time to campaign for the office of president of the Association of Presiding Presidents.

A "small vice" like alcohol or tobacco requires that we overcome an initial revulsion and dislike to achieve self-affirmation. Compulsory or obsessive hobbies, on the other hand, start out to serve as self-affirmation only to become an escape from a distasteful argument, situation, or task. We solve crossword puzzles as a distraction from worry; we go fishing to escape conflicts. We don't pamper our wives with jewels; we'd rather lavish that kind of attention on our sports car.

A hobby which has become habit or even compulsion is a farce of self-affirmation, an idol-role which serves as a defense and an escape from failure. Every time we fear a fiasco, adequacy, or inferiority, whether alone at home or else with others, a hobby becomes an excuse and an escape from a fear-situation.

We can regard as a "small vice" the *negative* hobby, and the *compulsive* hobby as a "positive vice." Since they are related, we can only differentiate between them by external, social criteria: health-damaging alcoholism is a vice, relationship-damaging "joining" is a hobby.

Spare time is the last bastion of freedom; it should be free of defensive fear and compensating idol-roles. It should be free of the need for any concessions, and lead to self-realization. It should find fulfillment in the satisfaction of genuine needs, in the reality of living itself. Self-realization must occur in the three areas of principal needs, e.g. body, soul, and mind.

Every hobby which satisfies the harmonious balance between these three ingredients, and which serves to develop a person's capacity in them (which would otherwise atrophy in daily drudgery), leads to that sought-after self-realization. *That* hobby affects the individual's existence, consumption and functions.

The Need to Exist

The basic needs the body must satisfy to exist and function are warmth, nourishment, elimination, exercise, and rest. Self-realization is impossible if even *one* of these requirements remains unfulfilled —as in the case with that half of humanity acutely threatened by hunger or stress.

The Need to Consume

The second area of need is "emotional consuming"—not merely the need to exist or to take nourishment, but the *enjoyment* of it all. We can satisfy hunger and thirst with potatoes and water. But to exist using all our senses and sensations, we'd rather try a Chinese appetizer, an Argentine steak with French sauce, a Bordeaux wine alongside Normandie cheese, and a Danish dessert.

We are captivated by the leaps of a gazelle, the crystal-pure singing voice of "the queen of the night" in Mozart's *Magic Flute*. We're exuberant over the bubbling noise of a ship's propeller, and we imagine ourselves in heaven upon hearing the soft and sonorous tones of the Signoria in *Firenze*. We drink in the glorious fall colors of a forest and are in-ebriated by the delicate fragrance of our beloved.

Emotional consuming is possible of every pleasant sensation perceived with out tongue, eyes, nose, ear ... and by our tenderness-yearning skin surface.

The Need to Function

A third area concerns the intellectual images our brain can structure, combining various concepts into plausible relationships. Thus a child draws a house, the research chemist designs a structural formula, and Mr. Smith looks up Mr. Jones in the phone directory, according to alphabetical order.

The Need to Reflect

If you *exist* well because milk and honey are abundantly available to you, you should feel satisfied. But it doesn't make you a *complete* person.

If you *function* well, and you manage to operate a conveyor belt, a computer, or a corporation, you may consider yourself useful. But it doesn't make you a *complete* person.

But if you *live consciously*, if you try to fathom reality and ponder the sense of your actions, if you're familiar with the meaning of right and responsibility, happiness and tragedy, love and death, then indeed you may consider yourself a *complete person*. You live according to your convictions; you live in human dignity.

In living constructively within the scope of our four needs, we achieve the level of self-realization.

In the proper utilization of our leisure time, we answer unfulfilled needs by the proper balance of these four areas. If, however, a hobby turns into habitual compulsion, we are nourishing an idol-role which negates self-realization. Since a hobby must satisfy at least *one* of the four areas of need—and finds expression within the four modes of behavior (Blue, Green, Red, Yellow)—we arrive at a systematic classification in four times four (sixteen) spheres.

The majority of hobby roles satisfy simultaneously two or more of these sixteen spheres or fields.

Dressage (a series of complicated maneuvers on horseback), for example, requires intensive physical concentration (vegetative +Green), subtle and tense attention, a concentration of all bodily moves and functions, and an authoritarian transference to the horse. At the same time, mastering of this noble sport involves an expression of prestige (consumately +Green). Golf requires at one and the same time prestige (+Green), physical concentration (+Green), as well as a substantial measure of hiking pleasure (i.e., wanderlust; +Red).

Hobby of the "Blue Type" (+Blue)

The "Blue Type" seeks satisfaction, relaxation, and peace. The hobby-signal of this type, in relation to physical comfort, is the horizontal mode of living —in reclining chairs, atop an air mattress, ashore or afloat, in a turkish bath, or preferably in bed, especially when we're depressed and self-pitying or daydreaming of our idols. Then we welcome a massage, a manicure; we like to be pampered and spoiled.

When we arise our consuming needs are activated. We become a hobby-chef, travelling any distance to discover a gourmet table. We take up painting or ceramics. Music appreciation or participation can become our major leisure activity. An avid fisherman, we're actually more interested in peace and quiet than in the scanty meal some lone, starved trout provides. Even the crack shot who only counts bull's-eyes subconsciously concentrates all his efforts on achieving emotion harmony.

The "Blue Type," however, is also capable of avoiding such emotional involvement, and surrenders instead to a peaceful and quasi-detached hobby. He or she experiences the universe as an empty bag, devoid of goodies, wonders, and miracles. With patience and great care that person collects stamps, petrified objects, minerals, antiques, butterflies, coins ... in short, everything that represents a cohesive series.

However, collectors who like to show off their possessions, whether shrewd "collector-thieves" who steal ashtrays or street signs, or speculators who displays their collections with the same emotion as if they were dollar bills or antiques, want to prove their superiority and nothing more.

The Hobby of the "Green Type" (+Green)

The living tactics of our "Green Type" consist in asserting himself in order to excel. That individual expresses this commitment in physical training and performance sports. His fundamental needs are the chronometer and the countdown. He is the scape-goat of hobbyists, responsible for the dripping vanity so evident in the sports world.

The ego-thriving "Green Type" is in his element when it comes to "living his hobby." Everything that can decorate and embellish his person is indulged in his hobby: clothes, shoes, hats, jewelry. But because he can wear only one hat and one pair of shoes at a time, he quickly arrives at a level where these decorative objects equal the opportunities to use them. Consumption then becomes a hobby and a purpose in itself, frequently in spite of other wants or needs.

Photography as a hobby nourishes a gigantic industry. Most frequently, "photography" means "me-photography." Me in front of the car, me in front of our house, me with my family, me in front of the Eiffel Tower, me on vacation. In any event, it's me in front of the camera, which creates a paper monument to my personality.

The most frequently practiced hobby and the most widespread "little vice" is one which occurs, as everything else that's self-evident, without a specific label or name. We'll refer to it as "hobby of expertise." In short, we're experts at such basic themes as weather, automobiles, comparative pricing, children, illness, political news of the day, restaurants and hotels, wine, vacations trips, and customs declarations. This is a matter of giving expert advice and judgment. Nobody questions it, nobody needs it, but practically everyone admires it. "It'll be nice tomorrow...I know a hotel near the Champs Elysées

where you can still get a room at moderate prices ...
If you want to eat the most exquisite spaghetti Na-
politaine, go to Chez Mario's in Oslo ... This vintage
wine must be stored at 56 degrees and savored at
precisely 54, that's when it's at its flavorful best ..."

The wine expert sniffs, tastes, gargles, and chews
the first swallow. With a patronizing nod, he declares that it's fit to drink; the rest he gulps down
like water.

If you're the classic hobbyist, you know at least
five jokes, one of which you'll change around to make
it appear brand-new.

All these so-called expertise-hobbies are signals
of an embarrassingly arrogant demand for affirmation, a yearning for recognition.

The "Green Type" seeks confirmation or recognition in his intellectual functions as well. He feels
like an exemplary scholar if he proves his "thought-
less" intelligence on a difficult crossword puzzle. If
he seeks peace and quiet and patience at the same
time, he'll solve monumental puzzles and confirm
(to no one in particular) that the chaotic universe
is a harmonious entity after all; a non sequitur at
best.

There's yet another kind of wordsmith, a hobby
poet. But he's the kind who insists on rhymes contrived at top speed and who cares more for the functional result than the emotional meaning of his
poem. His feelings are as meaningless as his verses.

At the highest level of functional intelligence,
we find the chessplayer-hobbyist. The amateur crafts-
man who wants to prove his manual expertise also

reinforces his esthetic judgment by using only the best materials and the most expensive paints.

The Hobby of the "Red Type" (+Red)

If you work during your leisure hours "by the sweat of your brow," you're the "Red Type."

Some reach for the lawnmower, the hedge trimmer, or even the spade to satisfy their need for physical motion. But since grass grows slowly and doesn't afford the chance to expend total physical energy, some "Red Types" take off on a strenuous hike, ridding themselves of excess strength in Mother Nature's domain.

Others work up a head of steam with the dog owner's trick, tossing a rock or a ball because that dumb animal believes he's got to fetch it.

There are many hobbies we gladly indulge in to balance our lack of physical activity in a desk-bound culture—tennis, football, swimming, bicycling, or working out in a well-equipped gym.

But what are the signals by which we can recognize whether it's a hobby to help us realize our physical potential, or merely a means of self-glorification?

If you indulge in sports to display your prowess like a model parading down a runway, you're not just doing it for self-realization and fulfillment, but to affirm your ego.

The clue here is the disguised need for an audience. It doesn't matter whether you're playing to spectators in the stands, showing off your skill on water skis, or just boarding a boat to display your captain's cap. Whenever we desire to make points with the public, timing laps in a race or wearing the latest sport fashions as a substitute for the pure enjoyment of exercise and body control, our hobby becomes nothing but a contrived self-affirmation. Sport becomes questionable publicity rather than enjoyment.

The tension and excitement the *active* sportsman experiences in his muscles occurs for the *passive* sports enthusiast—the spectator—inside him.

The motorcycle racer and the racing car driver do feel a physical strain, yet this tension (just as with the *passive* spectator) satisfies the emotional desire, the sensation-hunger.

The same yearning spawns whodunit stories, cowboy films, and sexually oriented pictures. They all build up a certain tension, which is finally released in an exchange of gunfire or another kind of confrontation.

In the same way, rhythmically accented music and fast tempos produce a state of excitement which can be measured or detected in a quickened pulse.

Even the heartbeat of bandmembers takes on a rhythm responsive to the beat of the percussion section. A detective story doesn't only produce excitement and tension, but demands a certain amount of intellectual problem-solving as well, thus taxing man's "gray matter."

Intellectual functions that excite tension without emotional involvement are a most welcome state of mind. The same satisfaction a game of solitaire or bridge provides a bored female, the pleasure a game of gin gives a male patron in a local bar—that same sensation pervades a sophisticated bigshot when he gambles on the market.

Every game satisfies a specific role. If we uncover it, we understand the meaning of the play-signals; we also realize the compulsion under which the hobbyist labors.

The Hobby of the "Yellow Type"

There are few leisure time activities designed to effect physical relaxation as a counterpart to continuous tension. Daily rhythm gymnastics are like poor relatives of great spectator sports like football or boxing. Only the pretense of social (i.e., contact) dancing will induce more people to indulge in loosening-up exercises. If we don't have much faith in flirting at a dance, we're apt to prefer loosening-up with alcohol.

Swimming, leisurely bobbing on the water, and drifting in a boat are among the few sports conducive to mental exercise and a state of relaxation. A penchant for easy water sports is regarded as a hobby-signal of a need to relax, unwind, and rest.

A connection between the physical and emotional feeling of a liberating release is found in the hobby of flying, especially in aerial acrobatics. But if flying becomes an obsessive escape from earthly pressures, then, as in compulsive auto racing, there is no longer a real goal or target in sight.

Every hobby which aims for new adventures is

a signal of the "Yellow Type." Curiosity is expressed in the urge to travel, in the need to be stimulated by a travelogue. Similarly, a visit to art exhibits satisfies the allure-curiosity. However, attending an opening at a gallery or a museum is less a matter of *seeing* than of *being seen*. It's not just a showing of pictures, but an exhibition of the visitors' culture, their thirst for contact and their desire to show off.

In the realm of the intellect, the "Yellow Type" expresses the reaction of a firecracker; one never knows precisely when and where it'll go off. Jumping from place to place, from one novelty to another, one relationship to the next, is symbolic of all hobbies of this type. The twentieth century was made to order for the "Yellow Type." He needs forty-eight hours a day and a telephone. "Making a connection" fascinates him or her. He travels, flies, often pilots his own plane. A steady stream of information and activity keeps him going, as electricity keeps a fan whirling. He loves to hear and pass along information on top of information: "You simply *must* read this . . . Can you give me a short summary of this?"

The signal of the egocentric "Yellow Type," who avoids emotional liaisons, is the search for contacts on purely professional or social grounds—encounters without emotional participation. "Yellow" functionals consider themselves the "jet set." If they can afford it, they'll actually *own* a jet plane; if not, they fly a model plane and wear pilot's wings, just to be "in."

Curiosity masquerading as a need for information is satisfied in many instances by television or radio newscasts and by home delivery of the daily paper. But sticking your nose in a newspaper or periodical without establishing a direct connection with your own goals is merely "tickling" your curiosity. Digesting stacks of newspapers or periodicals with different titles but similar contents signals a reading hobby and self-delusion, nothing more.

A Dog as Hobby

Logic tells us that children resemble their parents. That dogs should somehow resemble their owners seems ironic at best.

This hobby-idol can accompany us on four legs or on four wheels. An owners dream dog or car is such a clear-cut reflection of his affection structure that both become easily interpreted signals.

The "Blue Type" is attracted to a good natured and docile Newfoundland dog or a St. Bernard.

The "Red Type" is reflected in his possession of an agressive wolfhound.

The "Green Type" finds his image in a Great Dane, which, to him, represents the generous dimensions of his own home.

The dog-idol of the "Yellow Type" is the independent, elegantly prancing greyhound.

There are enough breeds to satisfy every made-to-order dog-idol role. Following are a few examples, systematically arranged:

+Blue, +Green =   faithful and smart dachshund or Yorkshire terrier

+Red, +Yellow =   playful and lively collie

+Blue, +Red =	alert, loyal, and devoted German shepherd
+Green, +Yellow =	conceited, grandiose, elegant Afghan hound or noble borzoi
+Blue, +Yellow =	lively and attached poodle or spitz
+Red, +Green =	contrary and aggressive Doberman pinscher or German shepherd

The Car as Hobby

There are enough four-wheeled specimens to let everybody "live" his or her idol-car role. The "Blue Type" drives the dependable family coach. The "Red Type" races his Italian sports buggy. The "Green Type" "dresses up" in a noble British chassis, and the "Yellow Type" needs a fast convertible. Preferred makes the idol-characteristics vary from country to country. Common to all seems to be the noble dignity of a Rolls-Royce or Bentley, the fashionable class of the Ferrari, and the sporty elegance of the Jaguar.

The VW "bug" impresses us as a dependable passenger car; minus its turtle-top, the wide-open convertible exposes its driver to the invigorating aromas of Mother Nature.

But, involuntarily, the "bug" owner has to watch the youthfully sporty Porsche and the elegant and fleet BMW pass him on the highways. Except for the dignified, utilitarian Mercedes, a U.S.-build car, luxurious and sensuous, indicates the "bonus uses" of an automobile. Yet in city traffic all cars are equal, especially when they all have to stop for a traffic light. The difference is in their image. And that is the signal which the car hobbyist acquires.

Chapter 9

Home Furnishings—Revealing Security

Louis XIV, the sun-king, needed the Palace of Versailles to feel comfortable. Diogenes, the sun-worshipper, felt at home in a barrel, and discarded his cup when he realized he could drink from his hands. Home furnishings are often explicitly symbolic of the inhabitant, of the person's style of living and the role he or she intends to portray.

The dimensions and shape of the room, the materials and manner of decoration are telltale signs, of essential parts of one's personality: sometimes shamelessly indiscreet (a framed diploma), frequently apparent trivialities (an overflowing shoe rack or a dusty plastic rose).

The form, shape, or dimension of the room,

whenever possible the architectural arrangement of space, and interior decorative details are adapted to the personal taste and needs of the owner.

The "Blue Type," who finds a comfortable home as essential as a fish finds water, needs an inner space expressing safety and security in tangible shape. He likes the grottolike room, rounded walls, and niches to which he can retreat and "nestle." He likes the dining nook with lowered ceiling, the round table around which people can sit in equality. The reading nook motivates him to read; the sleeping alcove induces him to draw the curtain. He likes the low ceiling of a farm cottage, or the small windows of an old stone house with thick walls and vaulted construction. He loves stained glass windows, and when he finds antique and small, blistered window panes which shield the quiet inside from the lively exterior, he wallows in safety.

The "Yellow Type," however, can't find a room that's spacious and open enough to suit him. He wants large and uninterrupted window panes, preferably wall-to-wall and leading to the wide-open outside.

The "Green Type" needs rectangular space. The corners are aiming-points by which he orients himself, judges distance and proportion, gets his bearings, and feels orderly and secure. The ceiling must be high enough for the "Green Type" to carry his head erect, assume a straight posture, and let his self-confidence soar aloft.

The "Yellow Type" would feel hemmed in if the windows weren't high and wide, whereas the "Green Type" finds high windows exalted and dignified. A wrought-iron gate outside the windows increases his feeling of security while adding to his sense of distinction at the same time. He'd like the glass door with wrought-iron decoration for reasons of fashion alone.

The "Red Type" loves elongated rooms, long, pillared halls, long lobbies, corridors, and long walks through offices and anterooms leading to the big boss's hugh office; he has to traverse all that space to arrive at the dynamic executive's desk.

Interior Materials

The character of a room is determined not only by its color scheme, but materials and their construction as well. Floor covering is a major factor, whether stone, linoleum-covered, or carpeted, whether the carpeting is of a loose or tight weave, fluffy and high, or dense and low, loop or velour. All of these determinants are signals of the type of person who'll feel comfortable here.

The "Blue Type" prefers warm materials such as brown or natural woods and textiles that feel soft and, like wall hangings or tapestries, give an appearance of softness.

The "Green Type" prefers hard stone, most likely marble. A metal-trimmed door and metal ornaments impress him.

The "Yellow Type" is fascinated by anything glittering or transparent, preferring glass, mirrors, Plexiglass, and shiny metals such as chrome or silver.

The "Red Type" loves leather, all kinds of pelts on floors or walls, lamp shades, and even a belted and buckled wastebasket, ashtray, or a leather-covered barometer. It the sexually oriented "Red Type" requires the same soft coziness of the "Blue Type," he'll spread out an animal pelt as a signal of sexuality.

The Room Ornamentation

Once roof and framework are completed, the development of living space begins. We're not merely concerned with materials such as marble and mirrors (they are conclusive signals), but with utilitarian objects—a simple water faucet—or decorative ones —a gold-plated dolphin-shaped tap. We may be deciding on an ashtray which won't be just a "crematorium," but a magnificent mausoleum. There are useful flatirons of chrome and steel which are stored in the closet, while rusty, useless but decorative ones are displayed. Most people who furnish their home with a spinning wheel know more about a properly functioning carburetor than they do about spinning wool.

Every object which stands about (like the spinning wheel) and most objects hung from walls are designed as ornamentation for the eye of the visitor. The effect of these pictures, wallmaps, trophies, and antlers are as vital to the completion of a home as the purchase of a tool kit.

Everything displayed for the visitor's benefit is a role-signal. Everything we use to give us the feeling of safety and security in the home is revealed through ornamentation; it becomes an indiscreet strip tease of our soul, the fireworks of our personality signals.

Here, too, we are aided by the four basic types of functional psychology and their six combination-types. They help in creating order in an arsenal of comfort and vanity.

The "Blue Type" decorates his home with signals of the heart, flowers, and candles which telegraph charming and delightful, snug comfort.

The "Green Type" decorates with signals of money and authority.

His prestige signals are ostentatious paintings or pictures of his forefathers which cause the visitor to grudgingly admit: "Man, that's wealth!" or "This stinks of class!"

The "Red Type" exhibits signals of potency documenting his daring and physical fitness with a collection of trophies.

The "Yellow Type" brings home the air of the great, wide world displaying world signals such as maps, picture postcards, and souvenirs from around the globe—the Eiffel Tower in a thimble, or a pagoda built as a gazebo—places he's visited, or places he'd *like* to see.

There are purse signals such as candles, or like signals of the heart unpretentious religious pictures. Much more frequently, two or even three signals are blended together. Tapers in an expensive silver candelabra represent a single signal of heart and prestige. The emphasis may be on prestige; the candles simply gather dust in the holder, or they may have been briefly lit to blacken the wick just for an effect of prestige. Candles may even be lit for the dual effect of heart and masculinity, if they are meant for the secondary purpose of demonstrating lustful desire.

Weapons (+Red), curved Arab daggers, or hunting guns or rifles are clear-cut signals of potency. Hunting trophies—rhino horns, antlers, and stuffed animal heads—hung from the walls display the active role of our subject individual.

When wartime mementoes aren't tucked away in a closet, but openly displayed, we recognize these trophies as a combination signal of potency and prestige.

Candles (+Blue) are an unassuming signal of the heart and geniality when they're dripping from a wine or whiskey bottle. They can become a signal of heart and religiosity, or, in baroque magnificence, a signal of heart-prestige combination, or, in provocative sexuality, a signal of heart and potency. Similarly, a display of jewelry needs proper interpretation to understand the personal motives of the owner.

Frequently, a signal, or a combination of signals, may be evident from the object itself. Or it may be determined only in connection with other signals. The place of display also contributes to the proper interpretation of the desired effect or signal, whether it's outside the home or next to the entrance, the connecting hall from one area to another, in the living room which is a center of activity, or in the intimacy of the bedroom—it all contributes to the proper and definitive interpretation.

Objects placed on the mantle, the sideboard, or over the couch represent a "prestige altar." The head-

SIGNALS			
+Blue	Heart-signals (candle)	+Yellow	World-signals (souvenirs)
+Green	Prestige-signals (diploma)	+Red	Potency-signals (weapons)
SIGNAL GROUPS			
+Blue, +Green	Heart-prestige signals of nobleness (antiques)	+Red, +Yellow	World-potency signals of the man of the world (map of the world)
+Blue, +Yellow	Heart-world signals of culture (library)	+Red, +Green	Potency-prestige signals of masculinity (hunting trophies)
+Blue, +Red	Heart-potency signals of eroticism (exotic pelt)	+Green, +Yellow	Prestige-world signal of prominence (original piece of art)

board of a bed is a "heart altar" for religious, sentimental, or illusionary desires. Hallways and stair-
cases are used as "altars of potency" for antlers and
weapons.

World-signals, such as picture postcards from
faraway lands, often surround a place of work, im-
parting compulsion and restraint. Photos of relatives,
children, and grandchildren are frequently grouped
around world signals—telephone, television set, or
radio. Sometimes they're nestled around a vase and
appear (especially if the vase holds artificial flowers)
almost like an idyllic private cemetery.

To give you a perspective on the functional
psychology of arranged signals and signal-groups,
the above table denotes, after the idol symbol
"+", the criterion or symbol and an example in
brackets.

Heart-Signals of the "Blue Type" (+Blue)

The dominating heart signal of the older generations and the spiritually faithful is the religious wall
decorations. A thorough analysis (Sturzenegger,
Lang, and Bern, 1970) revealed that religious wall
decoration is rarely used by younger individuals,
especially in their living rooms, that only one-third
of religious Protestants are so inclined, and that
religious jewelry is rejected, especially by professional people. On the other hand, older Catholics do
display religious symbols in their homes, especially
in the bedroom. Often, these are crucifixes and pictures of Mary. Or, less frequently, reproductions of

Da Vinci's "Last Supper," Dürer's "Praying Hands," or biblical quotations.

Besides the heart-signals of the heavenly home, more mundane symbols embellish house and garden. We encounter mythological symbols of nature, helpful ghosts that greet us in front of the house—a gnome here, a little "Bambi" figure there, a darling little dog elsewhere, all made of the same plaster. Sometimes these figurines live in a wee castle, or the castle with the mountain lake beside it greet us from a painting above the sofa. We can also interpret as a heart-signal an engraving of the owner's native village.

When the sensitivity of one's nature (+Blue) is in accord with readiness to "signal" the world (+Yellow) and a certain universality of the spirit, we experience a harmonious and cultured whole. When heart and universe find each other, the home becomes the focus of a boundless and spirited entity; its signal is a well-stocked library.

On entering a strange home, cultured individuals are immediately attracted to the bookshelves. They'll want to browse through the books to discover an interesting new subject or title. Intentionally and involuntarily, titles and clues of use or disuse (dogeared pages or dust accumulation) give the visitor a fair picture of the owner.

The person who arranges his books by size, or by soft-cover versus genuine leather binding, or who hides a bottle of whisky in a fake classic, has undoubtedly gathered his culture in his vegetable garden or somewhere in outer space; he surely didn't gain it from his books. Antique leather bindings and first editions could easily be signals of literary vanity if such displays aren't balanced by contemporary, ingenious, sensitive and spirited literature.

Musical instruments (+Blue) or musical scores which are in use and lying about are signals of the heart.

If the home is strewn with newspaper clippings or record jackets representing musical idols, or if a Beethoven bust or a picture of Mozart, Chopin, Liszt, or Wagner greets you from a bookshelf or wall, we may assume that such adoration has taken on an idol character, and that the owner wants to be recognized in that role.

If we find pictures of poets or of spiritual greats and world leaders such as Buddha, Socrates, Spinoza, or John F. Kennedy, they're usually signals of the owner's emotional accord with such opinions molders and their contemplation of our world and the universe.

Aside from candles, which we find in almost every home, flowers are a further heart-signal. Here, too, the signal character changes with type and motif. For example:

Field or meadow bouquet	= "Open up my heart with joy sublime in our beauteous summertime"
Strawflowers	= studied geniality, easily cared for
Green plants	= much and long lasting for little money

Orchids, roses	= expensive, hence fashionable
Carnations with greens	= less dear, but flowers nonetheless
Flower arrangement	= manifestly aesthetic
Artificial flowers	= plastic heart signals

Prestige-Signals of the "Green Type" (+Green)

One-third of the homes in all social strata display artificial flowers. It proves how frequently signals of the heart (+Blue) are switched to signals of prestige (+Green). This occurs not only with flowers, but with candles and religious pictures as well. Artificial icons, expensive plastic Madonnas, or triptychs are used to impress as signals of prestige. The most humble citations ("Pray and Work" or *Ora et labora*) can become self-conscious prestige signals ("Noblesse Oblige" or "Only work will help to find us, Give us self-esteem, Break the chains that bind us, Make us what we seem.")

Most "lovely" or "nice" objects are on display as prestige-signals. The family crest which formerly graced a portal and today hangs above the apartment entrance, has become a mere prestige signal. The gallery of ancestral paintings, an original Master in a pompous frame, tin plates and tankards, ornamental flatware, china figurines, lace covers, and fancy pillows—they're all signals of the heart which have been changed to prestige-signals. Wherever we find Oriental rugs, royal-style furniture, and antiques and copper engravings, the visitor is supposed to be impressed by the heart-cum-prestige combination which supposedly denotes or pretends nobility and traditional, cultured taste.

When we find a grand piano near the fireplace and an antique grandfather clock, we know the score!

On a less pretentious level, we find collectors of advertising coasters and beer steins, which represents more of a heart- or pride-signal. In the case of the rock or butterfly collector, the heart-signal predominates; the collector of coins or clocks again presents the prestige-signal.

Family photos are a combination of heart and prestige as they face us from their oval frames. If the businessman displays his dear ones in a sterling silver frame on his office desk, it's evident that he wants to be seen as a faithful and responsible business partner.

Precious signals of prestige are diplomas, honorary testimonials, and other such documents—paper ID's displayed to attest to the owner's intellectual superiority.

Photos and clippings displayed on walls showing personalities shaking hands with the owner are overtly shameless prestige-signals. Self-indulgent portraits where the owner looks down upon us have the flowery name of narcissism.

Photos of one's own wedding are only half as narcissistic, because neither partner has the nerve to remove a sacred illusion.

Simple souls living functional lives regard consumption and enjoyment of luxury items as the very embodiment of prestige. A large Italian or Spanish doll with no use but decorating the sofa represents pure luxury and the highest prestige to such a soul.

Potency-Signals of the "Red Type" (+Red)

The heart signals can bridge the space between sensible comfort and sexual stimulus, becoming signals of potency. If the stereo wafts peaceful rhythms across the couch, we classify it as a heart-potency signal. Pictures of hot-blooded gypsy girls and racy flamenco dancers, native girl figurines with or without grass skirts, and cozy tiger, zebra, or lion skins, are signals of a wish for sexual adventures. Just as grandfather lost his senses viewing "The Rape of the Sabines," so the sex poster excites and stimulates the adolescent (and older person); it is the same signal.

Whether pictures of female flesh provoke rather conventionally, or unconventionally, as pornography does, they resemble each other as signals of potency.

Teddy bears and stuffed toys which children drag around as defenseless victims of tenderness, or as bed partners, are erotic-signals. Dolls and mascots which ride on the car's dashboard are either heart signals or they're sexual potency signals (like death masks, skulls, or gnarled wood carvings).

Potency-signals (+Red) don't attest to actual sexual potency, but merely that we want to be seen as intense, stimulating, interesting, and desirable.

These glorified masculine traits are expressed through trophies, cups, and wreaths given by the bowling association, the ladies' club, rifle clubs, equestrian groups, soccer groups, or by the organizers of stock car competitions. Once at home, the silver-plated candelabra attest for eternity to the owner's strength, endurance, and splendor.

A child satisfies yearnings and moods by a massive display of miniature car models. A "big child" uses pictures and models of motorbikes, new or antique automobiles, or accessories that can double as indoor utility items.

Leather-covered containers such as wastebaskets, ashtrays, or whisky flasks from Spain all attest to the owner's masculinity. Add to that the world-signal of distant lands and you've got a man of the world indeed.

The important businessman displays a world map with position pins in direct line of a visitor's vision. If he's the skipper of a yawl, or a South Sea romantic, he'll moor at home between signal flags, hawsers, ships' lanterns, lifesavers, fishing nets, seashells, and a ship's barometer.

A world-beater festoons his walls with far-reaching signals of potency—shields and spears from foreign lands, a snake skin, and a gruesome crocodile.

The more modern conqueror of the world imagines himself as conqueror of the universe. He's exchanged his sailboat for a spaceship. The wind has been replaced by rocket fuel, hence a jet plane and a rocket model have replaced the former signal of "world potency."

Worldwide-Signals of the "Yellow Type" (+Yellow)

Besides geographical spaces, we would consider our subject's mental horizon. World-embracing intelligence (+Yellow) is a much-desired prestige-signal. It makes for the modern yet dissonant world-prestige accord. The desire for wealth and fame, to be "in," and to belong to the local "jet set" is an undemanding desire of minuscule importance. All signals which point to modernity, necessity, importance, and a vast circle of acquaintances may be confined to car, house, and garden.

Modernity may be expressed through modern art, from an original graphic to a stylistic arrangement on the living room floor which can become a topic of conversation when there's a lull at a cocktail party. The indispensability of one's personality can be documented by the arrangement of telephones throughout the house and elsewhere. Special colors, special answering devices in numerous locations—in the car, the garden, in all work areas, in the dining room, the bedroom, bathroom, and even in the private elevator. They all help to make decisions promptly if they're considered vital. A network of automatic equipment is found throughout the house, from the garage-door opener to a jet stream in the pool: doors, windows, venetian blinds, and even a manicure gadget—they're all automated.

A collection of menus from internationally famous spots, or a well-stocked wine cellar and tall bar stools which give guests the opportunity to assert their status to each other all add up to an inventory of world-prestige signals which lend dignity to the role-playing.

Chapter 10

Signals of Physical Complaints

"How's it going?" is a polite question which can ignore or satisfy with an equally short, "thanks." However, some of us take the question and ourselves sufficiently seriously to acknowledge it with "I can't complain." Still others can and do complain. They've got complaints, to be sure.

But complaints, even if they appear painful or are accompanied with lamentations, are not a reliable gauge of physical well-being. There are borderline cases where a patient complains of pain, but is organically healthy, and then there are cases in which an individual with no complaint, feeling healthy and seeing no cause to consult a physician, develops symptoms in need of clinical attention.

Each part of the human body transmits signals which constantly inform the human being of the state of his health. Depending on the attention a person devotes to his surroundings or to his own state of health, he is cognizant of his condition intensely, moderately, or not at all.

If we injure ourselves while our attention is occupied by another external matter, we are later astonished to find a bleeding wound which caused us neither sensation or pain.

Conversely, fear of a coronary pain or an asthma attack or colic can release in us these acute sensations quite spontaneously.

The individual who becomes a total realist will achieve a sober position regarding the world around him, as well as his own body. He perceives hunger and its appropriate satiation, and reacts properly to slake his thirst as well. He perceives fatigue, and he knows how to satisfy his need for rest and recovery.

The body is an important part of our realization of the self. Many methods serve this ultimate goal. On the one hand, we find sensory-motor training, and on the other, the autognostic regimen of yoga, whether Hatha-Yoga (on the sporty side) or meditative yoga, which cultivates both disciplines.

The corporeal realization of the self—our natural creativity—will escape us if we are dominated by our excessive demands, our idol-roles, or defensive-roles. In fact, our physical well-being will suffer if we submit to these conditions. We frequently cause ourselves to become ill. Weizsaecker declares that health is related to reality and truth, and illness is tied to unreality and untruth, to sham.

The more our psychic energy leans toward the idol-me and the fear-ego—as in depression and melancholy—instead of the real world of egocentricity, the more we dramatize the realistic condition of our own body. The body then plays a dramatized role, is forced to personify the dramatic complaints of the idol-role and the defensive-role.

The precise analysis of effect structure in the case of psychosomatic illness by means of the "clinical color test" (Test Publishers, Basel, Switzerland), has proven over the past two decades that for every "compensating posture" (i.e., neurosis) the idol-me is equal to a defensive-role, and the fear-me produces an idol-role. This may be determined by the compensating color preference (+), while the defensive-role is evident from the compensating refusal of a color (−).

Between self-reliance and the posture which depends on one's surroundings, there is a diagonal or crosswise relation; from the idol-me (+) to the defensive-role (−), and from the fear-me (−) to the idol-ego (+). Even though specific-effect structures with specific complaints in specific bodily areas or organs appear typical, no reliable causal determination of affected organs is possible.

If we compare the psychic conflict situation with an imminent thunderstorm, and expect that lightning will hit the lightning rod, or, practically speaking, if we expect that dammed-up aggression will cause an increase in our blood pressure, we simply assume that it all follows some rule of thumb. However, lightning frequently strikes next to a lightning rod, and accumulated aggression does not result in hypertension, but rather in an ulcer. In that case, an organic weakness already existed and offered an easy target. Subject to certain exceptions, we are now going to describe some psychosomatic physical complaints as typical signals of specific emotional structures.

Physical Complaints of the "Blue Type"

The basic theme of the life of the "Blue Type" is the emotional commitment, the relationship to a partner and his or her emotions. The partner's pendulum swings between an idol-role (+Blue) and a defensive-role (—Blue).

Idol-Role (+Blue)	Defensive-Role (—Blue)
need of rest	warding off lack of allure
intense need of emotional satisfaction and association	empty liaison, unrest
striving for harmony, sensitivity	blocking emotional surrender, turning away from partner

The complaints of the "Blue Type" are variations of a basic theme: his or her temper. This type's main ailments are temperamental ones—depressions. Midnight blue, in which this type sees himself drowning, is the typical color of depressive depths. Patients with agitated depression (+Yellow, —Blue) mostly prefer yellow and reject deep dark blue.

We can deduce the symptoms of agitated depression from: rejection of blue (—Blue) denoting fear of an attraction-void and of depressing boredom, which in turn causes unrest and agitation. A preference for yellow (+Yellow) indicates an exaggerated need for change, hope, seeking, drive. Which, then, are the motives for this idol- and defensive-role?

According to functional psychology, the defensive-role (—Blue) is linked with the idol-ego (+Blue). The demands of the idol-me (+ Blue) are excessive need for satisfaction, fulfillment, and a harmonious restfulness. Functional psychology further links the idol-role (+Yellow) with the fear-me (—Yellow): the fear-me fears expanse, being lost, and losing. Agitated depression (+Yellow, —Blue) which is manifest in disquiet, desperation, and an innate drive to escape from problems, has its roots in self-reliance (+Blue, —Yellow) which in turn grows out of fear of being lost and the yearning for shelter.

What begins as desperation (+Yellow, —Red) and a hopeless situation, slowly becomes in most instances a condition of acceptance. Displeasure and discomfort become habit. The idol-me resigns himself (—Red), but physically continues to play a defensive-role against a disappointing, senseless, and lost life (—Yellow). The depression (+Blue) is no longer physically evident; it becomes covert, masked.

This masked depression can now only be recognized by typical complaints: gagging feeling in the throat, tightness in the chest, difficult breathing, loss of appetite, feelings of anguish and anxiety, excessive perspiration, trembling, disturbed sleep, totally negative feelings, rapid exhaustion, and cool or pale skin color.

The depression (+Blue) can become manifest in one's vision: one sees everything through a fog— slightly fuzzy.

In the case of inhibited depression (+Yellow, —Green), the idol-me demands a self-aggrandizing superiority (+Green). The fear-me, on the other hand, is likewise dominated by a phobia of being lost (—Yellow).

Sleeplessness (—Blue), trouble falling asleep, and disturbed sleep are the most frequent complaints in the realm of the blue signal. The skin, an organ of tender emotions, similarly belongs to the blue realm. Sweaty palms and excessive sensitivity to cold or warm is an expression of unsatisfied, un- fulfilled, emotional relationship (—Blue) and there- fore inordinate tension and sensitivity.

Even more intense dissatisfaction (—Blue) and inner irritability can become manifest as itching or allergy. Blushing from embarrassment, becoming pale, or breaking out in perspiration are as direct manifestations of emotional conditions. Eczema of the genitals and painful constriction of the vaginal opening are frequently the direct result of a partner's rejection (—Blue). Allergies occurring in one's pro- fessional functions may be traced to rejection of some professional liaison (—Blue). Acne may result or multiply when tension and conflict occur with parents or one's love partner; this then reflects un- requited emotion (—Blue) which is often evident in young people.

Menstruating, which in a relaxed state is devoid

of pain, can become painful and disrupted or disturbed (dysmenorrhea) in case of tension (—Blue). In the event of conflicting sex relations (—Blue), it can become prolonged (menorrhagia), or fail to appear altogether and demonstate total absence of partnership relations. Alcoholism (+Blue, —Yellow) and obesity (+Blue, —Yellow) are a psychosomatic compensation for expectations (+Yellow) which have turned into disappointments (—Yellow) and which seek satisfaction (+Blue) in anesthetizing through alcohol or gluttony.

Physical Complaints of the "Green Type"

The basic theme in the life of the "Green Type" is realization of the self, his me-evaluation and his will. His problems swing between the idol-role of superiority (+Green) and the defensive-role against being the underdog, inferior (—Green).

Idol-Role (+Green)	Defensive-Role (—Green)
the will to assert	warding off narrow straits
the will-tension	obstacles against self-realization
the need to be in authority	tension of defensiveness
autistic role-demands	suffering under pressure, harshness or compulsive situation

The complaints of the "Green Type" are variations of his basic theme of asserting himself, taking hold of something or someone. What he demands, he wants to own or dispose of, and he'll defend his claim with all his might.

The spinal column, from the neck and shoulders of the small of the back is, in physical language, the embodiment of assertiveness.

The digestive tract—the pharynx, stomach, duodenum, gall bladder, great gut, and the anus—seem to describe in physical language how one conquers one's world. "Stubborn" is a descriptive word used in assertiveness (+Green) to the extreme.

Constant, barely perceived shrugging of shoulders as a means of assertiveness and defensive posture causes the neck and shoulder muscle of many individuals to constrict, cramp, and become sensitive to pain when one presses against them with the thumb. This constant cramp-posture can lead to irregular blood supply and severe headaches.

An X-ray picture may show vertebrae with damaged discs which may not feel painful to one patient. Conversely, we may find apparently healthy discs in a patient complaining of severe backaches.

A sensitivity to pain or pressure on the spinal column may not necessarily result from carrying heavy loads; it may derive from the psychologically defensive and assertive posture.

Constant defensive tension (—Green) against a life situation which we feel as pressure may result in a strong and persistent tensing of our back muscles which can result in pain and even physical damage.

In the lower part of the spine, the small of the

back (which can become sensitized during menstruation) engenders complaints caused by subconscious defensive tension (—Green) against one's own sexuality and sensuality.

Such defensive tension (—Green) exists in all cases where sexuality and sensuality are considered impulsive and inferior. This sensation is evident among all individuals whose assertive needs and me-idol (+Green) are a defense against sexual urges.

The digestive tract is the second arena causing frequent complaints in the physical language of the "Green Type." This area experiences not only the personification of the emotions of assertiveness (+Green), but physical manifestations as well. It wants to dominate that portion completely (+Green). The "Green Type" thereby develops activities by which he shares in the "Red Type" (+Red) as well.

Peculiar positioning of the teeth caused by constant tongue pressure may have been influenced by assertiveness and the will to dominate (+Green, +Red) or by lack of steadfastness and indecisiveness (—Green).

The pharynx can be defensive—evoke a choking sensation (—Green) if the me-idol (+Green) refuses to swallow what is demanded of it, feeling a situation depressing or insufferable.

The stomach behaves similarly. If the me-idol demands an unlimited success-horizon (+Green, +Red), a limiting or constricting situation may produce a defensive nausea (—Green) and vomiting. Such causes may be grounded in an unwanted pregnancy or a frustrating marriage situation; all of these irritate the me-idol (+Green) who may not be prepared to go on.

If the fear-ego suffers a sensation of inferiority and insfficiency (—Green) the stomach may play the idol-role of superior self-conquest (+Green). It pretends to be the ambitious devourer of everything, and thereby produces so much gastric acid that stomach pains and ulcers may result.

Experiments have proven that ulcers may be healed through psychologically effective sedation, a psychologic shield. We mustn't overlook the fact that such pharmaceuticals deal only with the acute symptom. Similarly, inflammations which cause duodenal ulcers or colitis can also be physical signals of a complaint. In these "soft" parts of the body, the assertiveness of the "Green Type" seeks to combine with the soft properties of the "Blue Type" (+Blue, +Green).

If the special demands (+Blue, +Green) of the idol-me are ignored, when loving recognition and personal esteem are omitted, the situation is felt as one of duress (—Green) and an inner aversion takes place at the same time (—Blue). The sensation of being ignored or repressed (—Blue, —Green), is frequently verbalized with the basic epithet "shit." The intestines play an identical role; in body language or physical expression, this feeling results in diarrhea.

Many individuals who feel unimportant, whose apprehensive-id is expressed by secret self-doubt (—Green) but who need a large dose of affirmation, experience the opposite intestinal reaction. Intestines and anus represent a true picture of personality—

tightened, cramp like, the latter tries to retain its contents and thus defend its possession (+Green). Constipation is the medical term for this complaint signal of the body language. Since the anus stubbornly expresses guarded personality feelings (+ Green), it soon manifests hemorrhoids.

Gall bladder bile can produce gallstones and cause colic pains. Psychosomatic examination with the color test appears to indicate that gall bladder complaints can be caused by demand for possession and disposal (+Green), as well as by fear of disappointment and loss of property, authority, or influence (—Yellow), and even by repression of disappointment (—Yellow).

According to K. Beckmann ("Illnesses of Liver and Gall Bladder Passages," *Handbook for Internal Medicine*, p. 529, 1953), 30% of males and 40% of females carry gallstones without ever having experienced pain. On the other hand, surgery has proven that gall bladder colic can occur without the presence of stones as well. Just as common usage links "bitter vetch"—gall juice—with envy and bitter disappointment, so, in fact, does body language manifest the bitter disappointment (—Yellow) of self-assertion (+Green, —Yellow) with gall bladder complaints.

Physical Complaints of the "Red Type"

Red represents excitement and its translation into bodily motor functions, movement, and activity. Excitement and action are expressed physically as demand for success and experience. In the idol-role, this is accelerated (+Red) into an urge for experience and a restless yearning for success, even to a hectic industriousness. The defensive-role (—Red), on the other hand, is a warding-off of excitement and irritating influences and excessive demands.

Idol-Role (+Red)	Defensive Role (—Red)
urge to experience	fending-off of excessive irritants
hectice engagement	excessive demand to experience
	irritability from weakness

The vital dynamism and activity level are stimulated by the demand for success and expertise (+Red), and life functions—especially blood pressure—are increased (+Red).

The activity- and success-demands of the "Red Type" are great. If that type experiences opposition, and if environmental conditions for its idol-id are unsatisfactory, aggressiveness results. To live out such aggressions would have undesirable results. Instead, the defensive-role becomes an emergency brake; it stems the aggressions (—Red). The exciting combat therefore does not take place in the arena of external living but rather within the body itself; blood pressure rises and can turn into chronic hypertension. Hypertensive blood pressure now becomes the defensive-role, finding physical expression in weakness and helpless unconsciousness (—Green, —Red). The idol-id orders a retreat from the arena of everyday ordinary life.

It is known that on encountering a new sex partner, the idol-ego of virility (+Green, +Red) generates the defensive-role of powerlessness or helplessness (—Green, —Red). Impotence is a radical means of avoiding the intolerable role of superior masculinity. The question becomes one of being embarrassed or becoming an omnipotent demigod. The idol-ego decides on embarrassment. Females whose fear-ego is characterized by fear of insufficiency, and especially insecurity regarding males, assume the idol-role of superior assertiveness (+Green). They remain frigid through self-control or through conscious exertion to reach orgasm.

Self-sacrifice or listless frigidity—that's the question. The fear-ego elects frigidity (+Green, —Red) because it fears that surrender would unleash a compulsive dependency.

W. Eggert in a 1967 article in the periodical *Medizinische Welt* (*Medical World*), demonstrated that a disposition to cardiac infarction may be revealed in the application of Lüscher's Color Test. He detected among cardiac patients, several months before acuity and prior to typical EKG signals, a compensating preference for red and green (+Red, +Green). This documented the urge for self-assertiveness, with a concurrent and specific alternate color preference (following gray and brown). The latter revealed a resistance-poor, vital exhaustion. Consequently, the self-reliance of the cardiac-prone is well-defined (—Red, —Green) as tortuous and repressed fear of failure and, finally, as fear of inner independence.

Whether the escape into such a stress situation (+Red, +Green) is the result of forgetting a bitter disappointment (−Yellow) or a defense against sinking into a depressing void (−Blue), can be revealed by the colors which the patient will reject as unsympathetic.

Physical Complaints of the "Yellow Type"

Yellow, the wide expanse, corresponds to the body language of respiration—breathing. The theme of the "Yellow Type" is the development of the adventure-horizon, the willingness to change and the expectation of things to come. We may await good things (+Yellow), but we also fearfully await (−Yellow) malevolence. Between the two poles, between the idol-role (+Yellow) and the defensive-role (−Yellow), our problematic pendulum may swing to and fro.

Idol-Role (+Yellow)

Accepting a challenge to release inner tension, expectation of encounters, extending the developing horizon, drive, fleeing a problem, illusory hopes of the future.

Defensive-Role (−Yellow)

Warding off the expanding horizon, fear of being lost, fear of being rejected, of loss of importance, apprehension, anxious expectancy.

We experience the changeover from expanding to contracting, or being enclosed, in our own respiration. Expansion (+Yellow) and being closed in (−Yellow) are translated within the chest into a language of breathing, i.e., volumn and frequency of respiration become our emotional barometer. Pleasurable enthusiasm and delightful expectations (+Yellow) expand the chest. Bitter disappointments, apprehensive fear (−Yellow) of losing something or someone beloved, and sorrow constrict the chest as if in a nightmare. According to D.A. Williams ("Acta Allergica," 1958 12/76,) in about 70.2% of the 487 tested patients afflicted with bronchial asthma, emotional causes were a contributing factor, in addition to infectious and allergic symptoms.

Psychoanalytical examinations show that patients with breathing difficulty often sensed their father as a repressing authoritarian figure. As a result, the majority clung to their mothers. The trustful sympathy (+Blue) and the open-minded empathy of the mother (+Yellow), her loving, spoiling, caring (+Blue, +Yellow) presented a paradise of cheerfulness and confidence. It would be a deadly shock and a nightmare to lose mother's caring or to confront brutal reality, to lose this Shangri-la to a sense of adandonment and loneliness (−Blue, −Yellow). But this loss of mother's nest for common everyday reality is bound to come sooner or later. The spoiled and over-cared-for child simply isn't prepared for such a trauma. Because of his total dependence on mother's care (which manifests itself as a possessive and authoritarian concern) the child becomes unable to exercise the required assertiveness (+Red, +Green) and he or she persists in a sense of abandonment (−Blue, −Yellow), of loss (−Yellow), and the privation of love (−Blue).

The relationship between the functionally psychological structure of asthma (blue and yellow) and depression (blue and yellow) has been clinically observed as interchangeable with asthma and depression.

It is understandable, then, that we find asthmatics described as having symptoms of the eternally abandoned (−Blue, −Yellow), of forever worrying lest they lose the sympathy of others. Descriptive words would be: "no self-confidence, defenselessly immature, shy, lone, outsider, but obliging and courteous, feeling a need of maternal protection."

According to statistics established in 36,892 tested individuals, yellow is the only color the average one would reject when measured by the normal sequence of color choices. The rejection of yellow (−Yellow) is not solely the signal of excessive and widespread fear or apprehension of losing human relationships, of possessions, this feeling of bitter disappointment and abandonment (−Yellow) is not merely a partial manifestation of asthmatics, but is also part of the total picture of many psychosomatic illnesses.

However, psychosomatic symptoms require an understanding of individual effect-structure by the use of the Clinical Color Test which simultaneously indicates different therapies.

Epilogue

While observing my fellow men and describing their signals, I did not pose the Punch-and-Judy question: "Are you all here?" nor was I interested in moralizing on any personal conduct. This guided tour through the anthropological garden of signals is intended to generate understanding and tolerance of every possible personality and character trait.

I consider ideological moralizing a signal of inner repression and of unreal or aborted self-realization.

Understanding and cheerfulness, on the other hand, are characteristic of people who need no signals.

BASIC TYPES OF FUNCTIONAL PSYCHOLOGY

Me-Self-Reliance

Conduct vs. the Environment

Me-Idol (+)

(excessive self-assurance)

Idol-Role (+) "target" (the urge for.)

Demand: absolute (I want unconditionally)	+1	+2	+3	+4
	satisfaction	authority	experiencing	independence
	stupefaction	impress	excitement	search
	regression	position of prestige	temptation	flight from problem

Self-unreliance (=)

	Self-realization			
	=1	=2	=3	=4
Demand: relative (I would like)	quiet relaxation contentment	firmness persistence self-piloting	excitation motion activity	release change development

Defensive-Role (—) "warding off" (fear of…)

Me-Fear (—)
(undervalued self-reliance)

	—1	—2	—3	—4
Demand: absolutely not (I don't want under any circumstances)	void of allure boredom lack of love	narrowness dependence compulsion	excessive challenge disgust exhaustion	distance loss forlornness

MORE HELPFUL READING FROM WARNER BOOKS

**BIORHYTHM: A PERSONAL SCIENCE
NEW UPDATED EDITION**
by Bernard Gittelson　　　　　　　　　　*(F36-072, $3.50)*
Now, with this new edition, you can chart your biorhythms through
1982! Discover how human performance is determined by three cy-
cles which you can compute and predict in seconds, without math or
machinery. This book means the difference between failure and a
full, rich life where you control your own destiny according to the
laws of science.

BIORHYTHM COMPATIBILITY
by Mort Gale　　　　　　　　　　　　　　*(F81-555, $2.50)*
A proven, simple method of biorhythm charting. It enables you to
check out your chances for long-term happiness with someone who
attracts you...anticipate and forestall crises at home or at work...
make sure your marital or work partner will be compatible before you
make commitments.

BIOFEEDBACK
by Marvin Karlins and Lewis M. Andrews　　*(F92-200, $2.25)*
The first comprehensive book on a new technique that places the
power for change and control in the hands of the individual, and not
with an external authority. BIOFEEDBACK is an extraordinary technique which allows you to control the state of your health, happiness
and well-being solely through the power of your mind.

THE DREAMER'S DICTIONARY
by Lady Stearn Robinson & Tom Corbett　　*(F93-917, $2.95)*
If you have different dreams, chances are you'll find their meanings
here. Lady Stearn Robinson and mystic Tom Corbett have gathered
3,000 dream symbols and arranged them alphabetically for bedside
reference. THE DREAMER'S DICTIONARY is the most complete and
revealing guide to interpreting your dreams ever published.

MONEYLOVE
by Jerry Gillies　　　　　　　　　　　　　*(J91-009, $2.50)*
Here are amazing, practical techniques and exercises that will en-
able you to think, live, and spend your way into prosperity. It teaches
you how to quickly rethink self-defeating attitudes about money; how
to gain fresh insights into earning, spending, banking and investing;
how to love yourself, your work, and your life.